Managing Performance

IN LOCAL GOVERNMENT

Managing In Local Government Series

The Managing in Local Government Series has been designed with one objective in mind: to give local government managers clear, practical guidance on how to be more effective.

Managers in local government currently find themselves under increasing pressure to develop new skills to deal with the rapidly changing environment in which they work. Written by practitioners, each book in the series features real-life cases, tasks or self-testing exercises which will help readers to get to grips with the new management style required to be successful.

The first titles are:

Managing Communication in Local Government
Mark Fletcher

Managing in the New Local Government
Paul Corrigan, Mike Hayes and Paul Joyce

Managing Performance in Local Government
Noorzaman Rashid

Forthcoming titles are:

Managing People in Local Government
Brian Blundell and Dennis Roberts

Managing Working with the Public
Sue Goss

SERIES EDITORS

The series editors have both been senior managers in local government. **Paul Corrigan** has worked in economic development at the GLC, been Deputy Director of ILEAS's education social work services and was Head of Quality Management at the London Borough of Islington. He was lead consultant in the establishment of the Camden Education Department. In recent years he has worked as a management consultant in local government. **Paul Joyce** was employed as Chief Training Officer and Assistant Director of Personnel at the London Borough of Islington in the early 1990s. He is now Director of the Management Research Centre at the University of North London. Both editors have been involved in research on the management of local government, both being interested in applied research which is of use to those with responsibility for the success and effectiveness of local government.

Managing Performance

IN LOCAL GOVERNMENT

NOORZAMAN RASHID

Published in association with the
IDA Improvement and Development Agency

**KOGAN
PAGE**

First published in 1999

Apart from any fair dealing for the purposes of research or private study, or criticism or review, as permitted under the Copyright, Designs and Patents Act 1988, this publication may only be reproduced, stored or transmitted, in any form or by any means, with the prior permission in writing of the publishers, or in the case of reprographic reproduction in accordance with the terms and licences issued by the CLA. Enquiries concerning reproduction outside these terms should be sent to the publishers at the undermentioned address:

Kogan Page Limited
120 Pentonville Road
London N1 9JN

© Noorzaman Rashid, 1999

The right of Noorzaman Rashid to be identified as the author of this work has been asserted by him in accordance with the Copyright, Designs and Patents Act 1988.

British Library Cataloguing in Publication Data

A CIP record for this book is available from the British Library.

ISBN 0 7494 2915 1

Typeset by Jean Cussons Typesetting, Diss, Norfolk
Printed and bound by Biddles Ltd, Guildford and King's Lynn

Contents

Contents

Foreword

by Heather Rabbatts
CEO of the London Borough of Lambeth

The ability of local government to publicly manage its own performance is now crucial to its entire future. It used to appear so much simpler. Local government could believe that the electorate, through the voting system, could provide the necessary performance management of Council services. The last twenty years have demonstrated that this is far too simple. Local democracy in and of itself does not have the power to manage and improve performance.

The management of performance is a grinding daily task, which needs the skill and commitment of public service managers. Of course elected members can assist this process, but without active public service managers it cannot be achieved.

Recognizing the day to day hard work in performance management is an important development. All of us in local government can identify with the impatience that some colleagues have shown when asked to collect data about their services. They claim that, if there are any spare developmental resources then they should go on developing the service, not on collecting numbers about the service. On top of this local authorities have experienced the Audit Commission hitting them with performance indicators, many of which singularly fail to indicate performance.

Yet despite this the last few years has seen an important series of developments in performance management. Recently it has become clear that old ways of assessing performance on an ad hoc basis at individual, service and organizational levels are no longer relevant. The new local government environment requires managers to adopt much more coherent and holistic approaches for their mixed economy of service provision in a fast changing environment that demands quality, value for money and social justice.

At the same time, as it travels through the journey of modernization, local government is becoming revitalized. Essential for this transition is the requirement to involve not only existing service users, stakeholders and employees in setting performance targets, but future service users too.

As one of the 'Managing' titles in the new local government series, this book outlines a new holistic approach to managing performance. It is based on the experience of leading-edge managers across the public, private and community sectors from many different countries.

This book develops a new performance management framework as an all-embracing approach to the experience of management. The framework is a diagnostic tool for assessing where organizations currently are in terms of their performance management capability. At the same time the framework helps managers to plot a balanced course of action to take, recognizing that the approaches they adopt will contribute to shaping the culture of their organization(s).

This innovative and pragmatic approach is based on the assumption that every organization is unique in terms of the balance between its socio-economic, geographic, cultural and political environments etc., and therefore requires its own distinctive journey or set of approaches to become a 'high performance, modern local authority' organization. Choosing the right balance of approaches from a menu of techniques is critical for success.

Above all performance is something that must be managed. And this cannot just happen through a system, it must be managed by a manager. The best performance management system is worth nothing if the people who are running it do not take an active part in its development. The manager needs to pick up early signals from any system and act on them quickly, because once performance has started to decline it is hard to reverse its decline. Leading-edge managers will have to be restless in assessing and improving the performance of their staff.

For Nasreen, Suriyah and Jamahl

Acknowledgements

This book has been brought together with the help, encouragement and support of a wide range of friends and colleagues from around the world, who work inside and outside local government. Needless to say, the faithful and professional support of my wife Nasreen was invaluable.

In particular I would like to thank professors Paul Joyce, Paul Corrigan and John Benington, and David Schmidt, the Director of the Local Governance Learning Network in South Africa. They have all inspired me through their own work and determination. Monica Fogarty, my friend and close colleague, deserves a special mention, particularly for her support in testing out the new performance management framework.

Friends and colleagues who have contributed to bringing this book together include: Joy McLanaghan, Jody Lee Glover, Steven Holmes, Steve Lacey, Simon Lawrence, Barrie Parkinson, Helen Dawson, Ian Briggs and Warren Tonks.

I would also like to thank the LGMB (and the Improvement and Development Agency), LGA, other individuals and all of the local authorities who have provided me with material and case studies for the book.

1 The new local government management context

The new local government management environment now and for the millennium can be described as 'chaordic', a composite of 'chaos' and 'order'. The term was first coined by Dee Hock of VISA to characterize this very large organization, which provides 355 million people with 7.2 billion transactions exceeding $650 billion annually. VISA's power and functions are distributed to the maximum degree possible, its governance distributed, it is infinitely malleable and yet extremely durable, easily embracing diversity and change – it finds its own order in a chaotic world.

Local authorities around the world – in the UK, South Africa, Russia, Palestine, Japan are all contending with major socio-economic, political, technological and environmental shifts. This creates chaordic environments. Such disturbances impacting on the work of local government increasingly test the commitment, determination and creativity of managers. There is a new local government emerging, and a context without ready-supplied guidance on how to make it work.

The new local government management context is about the fertilization of ideas, thinking, tools and techniques from across the public, private and community sectors. A richness of collaboration in the 1990s has contributed to a new combination of management philosophies for the next decade, referred to throughout this book as 'next generation management'. Local government is no longer just public administration nor indeed public management. Local government is about civic leadership and governance.

Councils are no longer mere agencies for the provision of local services. They are part of the democratic infrastructure of society and as elected representative bodies they make critical choices, not only about the nature and level of local services, but also about the revitalization of their areas on behalf of the communities they represent.

The range of issues facing local authorities is far too long and complex to fit within traditional management and political structures of local Councils. Economic regeneration, health, crime prevention, sustainable development,

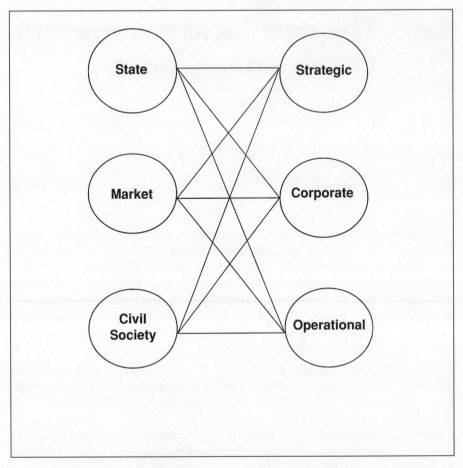

Figure 1.1   *Relationships for local government work (Benington, 1998)*

transport and education are issues that cannot be dealt with by single organizations or agencies on their own. They require a multi-level and multi-agency approach.

The powers and responsibilities of local authorities have been fragmented over the last two decades, and Councils increasingly need to synchronize and align their development of strategies and policies with others. This ensures that those who have a stake or indeed those who have a responsibility for spending public money network effectively, thereby ensuring that limited resources are used to best effect. The implications for local government managers and councillors are immense. Their ability to network in a multi-level and multi-agency dimension is paramount. Figure 1.2 is a network diagram illustrating the complexity of relationships between a Metropolitan Borough Council and a vast range of agencies and organizations.

Figure 1.2 *Network diagram of relationships (adapted from Alexander and Orr, LGMB, 1993)*

There is of course a parallel requirement in terms of how managers and councillors need to operate within their own Councils, across service areas and committees and across different levels of political and officer management. The local government environment in the new millennium is just far too complex and fast moving to work in the old style of local government.

At this moment you may be thinking of old style local government as bureaucratic and hierarchical with complex staffing structures and centralized departments. This is the very old local government. The old local government style that I refer to is that of the late 1980s and early 1990s based on matrix management working, loose partnerships and unconnected plans across the organization. This statement in itself is incredibly challenging and as we go through the book we can begin to see how what was appropriate management in the 1990s is no longer good enough for new local government in the new millennium.

Local government in the UK has a key imperative: to enhance its performance and to improve the quality of local services through its community leadership and governance roles. It is in this way that local government can become more relevant and revitalized in the eyes of citizens.

New local government will require leading-edge managers to focus on increasing performance through empowered people. These people will be both specialists and generalists, adding value to their contribution. Leading-edge managers will put a high premium on knowledge; they will share knowledge face-to-face and through electronic communication. They will operate in flexible work teams in both leadership and subordinate capacities, as the situation requires. Most importantly, they will work in service areas or business units across a wide range of agencies and sectors. How well managers are able to do this in the future will depend on the investment in their development, training and learning. This investment must be made right now both on an individual basis and by the Council.

New ways of working are needed to meet the key challenges of new local government the 'Third way' (Blair, 1998). Each of these challenges raises crucial questions about the skill and capacity of managers. To fully engage with them managers will need to develop new skills. The challenges facing new local government can be summarized as:

- local government's influencing role;
- the revitalization of local democracy;
- a mixed economy of service provision;
- the way in which local government views the public;
- the opening up of local government.

LOCAL GOVERNMENT'S INFLUENCING ROLE

Local government has over the past 20 years seen the erosion of its responsibilities to external agencies and arm's length organizations across different sectors. Traditional financial resources continue to be constrained, with any additional resources to be levered in through complex and sometimes incredibly bureaucratic bidding processes. To deliver their visions for their localities and achieve political priorities to meet local needs and expectations, elected members and managers will need to learn how best to influence others – particularly those who hold resources and themselves have power to make decisions.

Managers have to operate effectively across agencies and across sectors, building relationships with others to influence the development of strategies, policies and priorities and the allocation of resources. The performance of the Council can be measured by its success in getting others to align or synchronize their resources and energy to deliver agreed priorities and in turn meet the citizens' needs.

Approaches to influencing

- Cooperative – achieving shared aims and sharing resources. Often expressed in joint working groups, joint boards for transport, police, fire and civil defence.
- Negotiation – exchange of resources, favours, support for one another's initiatives and bids. This can even happen between organizations that do not necessarily have common interests and values.
- Campaigning/lobbying – adopted to openly oppose policies and actions to be pursued by others. There will always be a basic conflict of interest and values.
- Relationships – involves the local authority building close working relationships with other authorities or agencies to influence them to change policies or decisions, perhaps modifying their own actions, but not actively opposing.
- Adding value – the local authority facilitates the achievement of another authority's or agency's policies and/or actions. This will quite often happen where there is empathy with the issues and values of the organization concerned.

(Adapted from Stewart, 1988)

 Task 1.1

There are no hard-and-fast rules about how and when to use the approaches to influencing. Take a moment to think of a situation where you have had to influence an individual or organization. Which approach did you use? How successful was it? Which skills were involved?

THE REVITALIZATION OF LOCAL DEMOCRACY

The second key change in local government is the revitalization of democracy. I am sure you have often wondered how strongly individual citizens feel about local government and local democracy. The experience of local democracy, while it represents an opportunity for involvement for all adults in the process of government, is not very important to most people. Electoral turnouts are lower in Britain than in any other European country; active involvement in local politics is even smaller. Voting in local elections does not mean much to local people. In real terms it does not leave local people 'feeling in control' of local government. Rather they feel that 'the Council' is in control of them.

New local government recognizes that, however important elections are, there is an enormous democratic deficit in the relationship between town hall and local people which annual elections on their own cannot and do not fill.

In 1998 MORI interviewed a representative quota sample of 2017 adults. When asked about voting at Council elections, 24 per cent of the respondents said that they rarely voted (7.5 per cent) or never voted (16.5 per cent) in Council elections. 'New local government, therefore, has a restless search for local people to influence and participate in the way in which decisions are made about their lives' (Corrigan, 1999). It recognizes that the direct election of local councillors is the main and determining factor for democracy for local government. Yet, on its own, it has not provided sufficient experience of influence and control for local people to give them a grounding and belief in the fact that they run local government. The people do not see local councillors and chief officers as their servants, but rather as their masters and mistresses.

More recently local government has found new ways of involving local people in democratic decision making processes. These range from citizens juries to community panels and neighbourhood focus groups. In the future these ways of working (which for the purposes of this book will be termed 'community participation') will create an important pillar in establishing the next generation of management for local government. The work of managers in local government in the future will increasingly involve building relationships with service users and citizens to identify and discuss their needs, to involve them in monitoring and reviewing the performance of the services we have delivered or enabled and, most importantly, to involve them in scrutinizing policy while at the same time putting forward ideas for current and future priorities.

The Local Government Association (LGA) has established all-party support for five key commitments to contribute to the revitalization of local democracy. They are a sign of local government's determination to seek new ways of working for the millennium in order to respond to a changing society.

Commitment 1: Higher standards of probity

Measures include:

- Adherence to the five principles of public life established by the Committee for Standards in Public Life.
- A local code of conduct, as recommended by Lord Nolan.
- An open system for enforcing the code.

Commitment 2: Stronger community government and civic leadership

Measures include:

- Developing a shared vision for the area in partnership with the public, private and voluntary sectors.
- Making it clear to the public who is responsible for decisions.
- Ensuring local people's priorities are the Council's priorities, and giving every resident and local business the opportunity to comment on budget proposals.

Commitment 3: Delivery of quality services offering best value for money

Measures include:

- Publishing information to show we are securing year-on-year improvements in service quality and service cost.
- Publishing challenging local performance indicators and reporting against them.
- Consulting local people on priorities for service improvement.

Commitment 4: Renewing local democracy

Measures include:

- Increasing the proportion of people who are registered to vote.
- Improving local publicity about local elections and how to vote.
- Increasing the number of people who vote in local elections through developing new ways of voting.

Commitment 5: Modernizing the structures of local government

Measures include:

- Streamlining decision making and differentiating executive, representative and scrutiny roles for councillors.

- Opening up decision making to the public.
- Improving the responsiveness of the Council to the public, especially by telephone, and through improved use of information technology.

 Task 1.2

It is universally agreed that our public are both customers and citizens. From the list below describe what customers and citizens are entitled to or are interested in:

vote;
respect;
to be listened to;
quality standards;
fair treatment;
access to information;
know why decisions have been made;
review policies and performance;
pay for services;
reliability.

THE MIXED ECONOMY OF SERVICE PROVISION

The third key theme of change in local government is about why and how services are made and delivered for our communities. For years (in the UK at least) the proposition in local government has been that local authorities (particularly those that are Labour controlled) will employ staff directly to deliver services for the citizens in their localities. This proposition is no longer valid: local government cannot sustain the cost of providing and delivering services to meet growing needs and expectations within a continuously shrinking resource base. The argument for financial resource is a 'non-argument', as more resources would not necessarily lead to increased productivity, efficiency, effectiveness and quality. Rather, these resources would be used in traditional ways for solving problems of staff costs and support costs to service delivery units. In a growing and competitive environment, organizations in other sectors have looked for and found new ways of working across sectors to make and deliver services for our communities at lower cost and with better quality.

This fragmentation of local government services has and will continue to be managed by councillors and managers. However, new local government has a job to undertake in not only identifying the most efficient and effective means of service delivery, whether in-house or externally provided, but also in involving current and future service users in articulating their preferred delivery mechanism. In this sense next generation management in local government will require managers to understand more clearly market mechanisms, the ins and outs of joint ventures, trust status and the notion of strategic alliances, enabling them to pursue alternative delivery mechanisms when required. Allied to this will be the need to understand the external market: how it operates and how to work within that market while ensuring citizens get what they want. Within the family of local government organizations alternative delivery mechanisms can be achieved which often require the bundling of mixed packages of funding at local, regional, national and European level. These require a high level of sophistication in terms of performance management. Managers need to find multiple ways of enabling their services to be delivered for differing needs within diverse communities.

 Task 1.3

What does a mixed economy of service provision mean? In what ways other than in-house does your Council provide services?

New local government believes in a pluralism of service delivery. It takes control of the decisions about the service delivery mechanisms and ensures that they are made for each service in a specific way. For example, many social services departments will not have a single method of delivery for domiciliary care. Some parts of the care service will be delivered by local authority workers, others by health agencies, others by a voluntary agency and others by private agencies. All of these will be very specific contracts for very specific services and will meet the needs of the service delivery because of their different forms of service provision. 'The model of making decisions around specific services and different forms of delivery mechanisms is one of the highlights of the new form of local government' (Corrigan, 1999).

The removal of services to arm's length organizations and external agencies, for example the Careers Service, has already evolved a new set of competencies based around networking, influencing and negotiation. Managers in the future will need to increase their proficiency in these areas as the management of services becomes more and more complex across agencies and sectors, and further complicated by mixed packages of funding at a local, regional, national and even international level.

THE WAY IN WHICH LOCAL GOVERNMENT VIEWS THE PUBLIC

The fourth key theme of change is the difference in how local government views the public. Old local government was proud to see the public as citizens. It developed its relationship with local people through the citizenship relationship with the state. It saw local people as 'governing' the local authority through their right to vote and through their citizenship rights. However, citizens are also consumers and users of services. This in itself has caused some difficulty since it was felt that it would detract from the nature of the citizenship relationship.

There is no doubt that in local government there is a difficulty of language in terms of how we can express a very complex relationship between local government and citizens who are our electorate, consumers of our services and our customers. The implications for managers here are to do with how we relate to and view the individuals who use our services – or indeed do not.

THE OPENING UP OF LOCAL GOVERNMENT

The fifth key change emerging in local government is the way in which local government has become more open in recent years.

Whenever a local authority has become the object of criticism it has had a tendency to be defensive and to close itself off from the public. This does not lead to a good relationship between the public and the organization. New local government is about being open and honest in its relationships; this is not easy.

There are many examples of Councils opening up to the public. They include the publication of more details on performance against the priorities that are shared with the communities; scrutiny panels and select committees to look at issues the Councils are involved in; and the involvement of community representatives and individuals on Council committees both as advisers and as scrutineers.

The political need for honesty throws up some real challenges for managers in local government in that they must take on board the experience of honesty and openness. However, as much as we want to be open it is very difficult for managers to be totally honest about the nature of the issues and problems within their organizations. Quite often this is because of a blame culture, a lack of a learning organization approach to dealing with mistakes, poor performance and political indiscretion. It is even harder for private sector organizations to achieve this goal since they are bound by or believe they are bound by issues of commercial confidentially. Perhaps the first step in local government is to begin sharing within the organization itself how well it is or is not achieving its priorities and targets in meeting the needs of citizens, and then to begin to develop a similar relationship with citizens themselves.

 Task 1.4

Ask yourself the following questions. What information do you currently share with citizens? What information do you not share with citizens and why? Construct a mini action plan of areas that you would like to prioritize for sharing with citizens to help develop the openness of your service provision.

NEXT GENERATION MANAGEMENT – MANAGING THE CHANGE FROM OLD TO NEW

The transition from old to new local government will require a new set of abilities, skills and competencies. These changes are not easily understood through a summary of bullet point headings alone as they are all interrelated on many different levels.

The preceding paragraphs have given a snap-shot of the changes. However, to manage something as complex as our subject matter it is particularly helpful to illustrate management styles and ways of working of the last 20 years or so alongside the next generation management; Table 1.1 makes this comparison.

'Next generation management' is a term to describe the fertilization of ideas from across different sectors that have emerged as winning approaches for working in our chaordic environment in the new millennium. This does not necessarily mean that previous ways of working are now totally redundant. However, in using old management styles and approaches one must consider carefully their relevance to our new environment and whether or not by working in such ways we will prevent our local authorities from moving forward. The new high performance local authorities will continually evolve to meet the changing needs of the environment and their citizens. They are 'learning' Councils.

The 1990s saw a significant turning point for local government management, away from the 1970s 'command' ethos which was reflected in bureaucratic and hierarchical staffing structures; chief officers as barons, control communication; committees as the focus for Council activities; the 'do to citizens' approach rather than 'do for'; external liaison only where needed on professional matters; and a high level of attention on inputs. That era of bureaucracy rested upon a more stable environment and 'Fordist' approaches to production. Local government in the 1980s reflected a combination of styles and approaches, discussed below.

Table 1.1   *The changing face of management approaches*

1980s	1990s	2000 and beyond 'next generation management'
Near monopoly	Partnerships	Arm's length companies and joint ventures
		Strategic alliances
Compulsory competitive tendering	Purchaser-provider split	Best value
Hierarchical	Matrix management	Networked organizations and flexible work teams
Central control	Management by contract and influence	
Stable employment	Flexible employment structures	Cross-sectoral employment
Quality assurance	Total quality management	Business excellence model
	Excellence	
Personnel specification	Competency profiling	Intellectual capital
PRP	Staff appraisal	Succession planning and non-cash rewards
Equal opportunities	Social justice	Social inclusion and diversity
Neighbourhood and area working	One-stop shops	Call centres
		Electronic information
Community development	Community government	Citizen-centred government
Public meetings	Resident surveys	Community participation
Corporate management	Strategic management	Strategic control and influence

The competitive Council

A Council developing the business ethos, welcoming compulsory competitive tendering while considering other ways of outsourcing. It adopted business techniques, created business units, and changed from using local government language to private sector language. The competitive Council would also reflect a more streamlined committee structure focusing on strategic services where members see themselves as directors of the board. The driving force behind many improvements was to create short term savings with less thought for the long term future of the service.

The consumerist Council

The most dominant of this type of local authority had a fixation on satisfying the individual customer through the provision of a set of services. A strong emphasis for such Councils was the customer care programme. The main criticism of the consumerist approach was the imposed 'charm school' of smiles, badges, piped music and glossy in-house charters, leaving the fundamental questions of 'how' and 'responsibility' unanswered.

The community-based Council

These Councils focused on their role in terms of accountability to the citizens, realizing that this was as important as responsiveness to customers. They recognized that elected members had a role in monitoring services provided by the local authority as well as providing community leadership. The community-based Council was the beginning of an approach to working across sectors in partnership with others to make things happen for local people. It was the beginning of community participation.

These generalizations of the different types of Council in the 1980s reflect the turning point of local management, and are shown in Table 1.2. The 1990s saw a period of prolonged flux, innovation and uncertainty and an information technology revolution allowing for operational decentralization.

Local government management in the 1990s has learnt from the pros and cons of the approaches adopted in the 1980s. There has been a recognition that the 'excellence approach' advocated by Tom Peters and Robert Waterman was clearly relevant in terms of closeness to the customer, a bias for action and productivity through people. However, the whole debate about the role of local government in terms of civic leadership and governance was absent from the 'excellence approach'.

Next generation management

Next generation management is the cross-fertilization of ideas from different sectors, built up over the past 20 years. Next generation management is an attempt to repackage what was relevant from the past into what is more appropriate in the new local government environment.

Table 1.2 *Types of council (Usher and Darborne, 1993)*

COMMAND COUNCIL	COMPETITIVE COUNCIL
Hierarchical and bureaucratic control	Enabling not providing
Paternalistic attitude to customers	Streamlined structures
Committees all important	Fewer committees which monitor
Chief officers as barons	Business units
Emphasis on inputs	Statutory services only
	Cost-cutting focus
	Market led
CONSUMERIST COUNCIL	**COMMUNITY-BASED COUNCIL**
Customer oriented	Community involvement
Managerial orientation	Cross-sector working
'Charm school' and charters	Community advocate
Excellence philosophy	Partnership approach
More responsible, but no more accountable to citizens	Area working

Citizenship

Next generation management will look at the citizen as consumer and the consumer as citizen. There will be no boundaries, no fuzzy relationships; instead there will be clarity in terms of accountability for:

- probity (legal and financial scrutiny);
- process (observing procedures of the Council);
- performance (achieving efficiency, effectiveness and meeting social values);
- policy (judgement in terms of what is or is not needed).

Informing

Next generation management will ensure that citizens, whoever and wherever they are within their localities, have information about what is available to them in terms of services, advice and guidance. Information about the performance and priorities agreed for the Council, details of each service and which elected members and officers are responsible for them, will be readily available. As information and communication technology evolves and the costs are reduced, management will more readily be able to engage citizens through this technology.

Market intelligence

Next generation management will be concerned with what, why and how citizens want in terms of their quality of life and services the local authority has responsibility for providing or facilitating. Next generation managers will harness information and communication technologies to better understand the democratic profile and needs of citizens. Next generation management will also gather knowledge of alternative delivery mechanisms in the market place that are as good if not better than existing ones.

Social value

Next generation management puts a high value on issues of equality in terms of meeting the needs of a diverse community and including those who are most disadvantaged in our society. Next generation management will question how 'what we do' contributes to regenerating and developing the capacity of citizens we serve in a sustainable way.

Networked organizations

Next generation management will require both its councillors and managers to work across sectors and across teams, taking both leadership and subordinate responsibilities as appropriate. These teams are known as 'fractal' teams (see Chapter 9) and go beyond traditional matrix management.

Cross-sectoral employment

Next generation management will require more managers who are both specialists and generalists working in fractal teams across sectors, seeking contractual relationships in a range of organizations.

Strategic alliances

Next generation management will move away from softer partnerships to more performance-oriented relationships such as joint ventures and arm's length trusts to achieve their purpose and aims. Relationships will be nurtured well in advance of the fruition of such outcomes.

Best value

Next generation management will transfer learning from across sectors on total quality, value and performance management approaches (such as the Business Excellence Model) to the new local government environment. Best value, with its own performance management framework, will be the principal ethos for bringing together ideas about citizenship and customer.

Strategic foresight

Next generation management will recognize that the old ways of strategic planning (short term and ad hoc) based on building of scenarios is no longer apt. The emergence of information and communication technology to involve citizens, to gather trends and data and to analyse it will enable managers to more accurately pinpoint what will happen in the short and medium term. This will contribute to greater strategic control in terms of the direction of the organization and the overall allocation of resources.

 Task 1.5

Recap what is old local government and what is new local government. What do you need to do to adopt next generation management approaches?

SUMMARY

Chapter 1 has set out the new local government context, enabling the reader to develop an overview of the challenges for new local government and next generation management.

Chapter 2 will explain what we mean by performance management and its contribution to next generation management. Following chapters will examine in more detail how a new performance management framework can help to set new directions and balance your organization's approach to improving performance in a coherent and holistic way in the context of new local government.

REFERENCES

Alexander, A and Orr, K (1993) *Managing the Fragmented Authority*, LGMB, London.

Benington, J (1998) *Relationships For Local Government Work*, Warwick Business School, Local Government Centre, Coventry.

Blair, T (1998) *The Third Way*, The Labour Party, London.

Corrigan, P (1999) *Managing New Local Government*, Kogan Page, London.

Stewart, J (1988) *Understanding the Management of Local Government*, Longman, Harlow.

Usher, M and Darborne, B (1993) 'New approaches to governance and service delivery', *Local Government Policy Making*, 2, 2, October.

2 | Performance management explained

This chapter aims to help you to make a leap from traditional approaches of performance management to a more holistic approach relevant to new local government. Traditional and new definitions, and the challenges and reasons for performance management are shared in the first part of the chapter. The second part makes the connection to individual performance and examines the relevance of performance related pay. At the end of the chapter there is a system for testing your organization's high performing culture.

The language for performance management is not clearly developed. As the context of local government changes and the context of management across sectors changes and ways of working become increasingly complex and networked, the language we use needs to be redefined from time to time. Clarity of language will help us learn more quickly the processes, tools and techniques that are relevant to each and every individual local authority and its particular circumstances.

In the new local government environment, high performing, modern local authorities will see performance management as a multi-level and multi-arena activity. It links political and managerial strategy and service objectives to the needs and expectations of citizens, and the jobs of people across agencies that are responsible for meeting these needs. It involves monitoring and evaluating performance, feeding back into the system and learning how to bridge performance gaps.

Performance management is multi-level as it takes place at all levels in organizations, from chief executive to front-line operative. Performance management is also a multi-arena activity because it takes place around a range of arenas which are to do with citizens, political management, strategic planning, organizational performance, quality standards and operational frameworks (discussed in detail in Chapter 3).

THE TRADITIONAL DEFINITION OF
PERFORMANCE MANAGEMENT

The following definition of performance management reflects the most common aspects that are incorporated into traditional definitions:

Individual and organizational performance is integrated with a set of planning and review procedures which cascade down through the organization to provide a link between each individual and the overall strategy of the organization.

It could be argued that in the new local government context this over-simplified view of the cascading down of the link between organizational strategy and priorities to individuals is not adequate. This is because, we argue, new local government concerns reaching out to our citizens, listening more clearly to their needs, priorities, expectations, hopes and fears and cascading these upwards in to the organization in the first instance before the cascading downwards can begin. The first review in this process must involve the public setting the agenda for the organization to follow.

Performance review is described by the former Association of District Councils in their guide on the same subject:

It can involve setting policy objectives and measurable targets for their achievement. It requires the creation of uncomplicated key performance indicators and regular systematic review of results by reference to those indicators. Identification of indicators and the measurement of results provide the basis for review of performance of services compared with the targets and standards originally set.

This traditional view of performance review, acceptable in the early 1990s, does not go far enough for new local government and does not appear on the menu of next generation management techniques. It is too narrowly focused on the organization itself and does not acknowledge the shift towards multi-agency working across sectors which involves the levering in and influencing of resources to make things happen. It does not recognize the need to involve others: key stakeholders, other provider agencies and the community.

Traditional approaches to performance management link the strategy and service objectives of the authority to jobs and people. The approaches have been systematic and vary in degree of formal structure. The most detailed form is based on setting corporate, service, team and individual objectives; recognizing achievement; identifying training and development needs; then using the knowledge gained to modify objectives and methods as necessary.

Unfortunately such a systematic approach alone is no longer adequate. Aspects of the organization's ways of working or culture, systems and processes, control tools and (most importantly) involvement of citizens need to contribute to a more coherent and holistic approach to future performance management systems. A new framework for performance management for leading-edge local government managers has been developed, and is described in detail in Chapter 3.

Traditional approaches to performance management are about motivating staff by concentrating on priority objectives, raising commitment and releasing potential. Quite rightly they have focused on people rather than systems-dominated strategic planning processes. However, contemporary approaches have not gone far enough in terms of real people's contribution to performance based on their beliefs, values and personal commitment and behaviours. In later chapters we discuss how individuals and teams can be further developed to create high performing, modern local authorities.

What is performance management?

The Local Government Management Board's description in their guide to performance management (1994) is slightly more up-to-date:

> A means whereby accountability for contributing to the organization's strategic and/or operational objectives is allocated to employees and where these contributions are measured objectively.
>
> The outcomes are thus used to inform decisions about the further objectives and needs of the organization and its employees. The outcomes must match what members want, introduce or reinforce a performance culture and improve quality of services to customers.

PERFORMANCE MANAGEMENT: KEY TERMS AND DEFINITIONS

In developing your thinking and your authority's approach to performance management it will be helpful to have clarity and agreement on the terms and definitions used. The following list provides a range of terms and explanations you may find useful. As discussed earlier the language for performance management is inadequate. To help us move forward we can at least share some common terms and their definitions. Here is a selection from Fogarty (1998):

Aims: The general outcomes that are to be achieved through actions or activities.

Objectives: The specific overall impact that is to be achieved by undertaking specific actions or activities.

Targets:	A special task(s) that needs to be achieved over and above routine work.
Inputs:	The costs and resources used.
Outputs:	The goods and services provided.
Outcomes:	The impact (effects) of the services delivered. Measuring outcomes is generally recognized as difficult.
Economy:	The relationship of the outcome to a base using comparisons, eg, standards, estimates, forecasts.
Efficiency:	The relationship between inputs and outputs. Generally the aim is to maximize output with minimal input.
Value for money:	A measure of the contribution made by an activity/service focusing on economy and efficiency.
Evaluation:	The process of checking whether an organization is achieving the impact it intends.
Monitoring:	Keeping track of inputs and outputs – a rudimentary form of evaluation.
Benchmarking:	The process of measuring an organization/service performance against the performance of another organization which may be recognized as 'excellent' or 'best in class'.
Performance appraisal:	The activity of evaluating actual achievement against set targets or objectives. This is usually undertaken as part of an interview between employee and line manager.
Performance indicators:	Yardsticks used to assess the achievements of the results. In the main PIs should be objective and cover both quantitative and qualitative aspects.
Performance measures:	Used to quantify objectives and to assess achievement. They give an index of achievement and act as a judgement aid to consistency and fairness.
Performance review:	The comparison of actual results against the desired results expressed as a standard of performance.
Performance standard:	The agreed performance that is to be achieved. The aim of standards is to assist in setting desired levels of performance which can then be used to appraise actual achievement.
Values:	The fundamental principles that guide the way an organization operates, eg, quality, equality.
Social value:	The impact of an activity/service in terms of contribution to society. This may include contribution to things like quality, equality of opportunity, environmental issues.
Best value:	An emerging culture for local government arising out of central government legislation. Placing a statutory duty on authorities to secure economic, efficient and effective services.
Local performance plan:	An action plan drawn up by local authorities in consultation with communities/stakeholders, providing the common links between the principles of best value and the means by which local authorities will be held accountable for the quality and efficiency of their services.

Service improvement plan:	An action plan setting out details of the targeted improvements to be made to a service/performance. The plan is usually the result of feedback from stakeholders on current, actual performance and the acceptable level (or not) of this performance.
Community plan:	Involving local communities, businesses and stakeholders in the process of settiing service targets for the local authority. This includes defining priorities and objectives and agreeing acceptable measures of success. Ideally, the community will also hold the council accountable for its progress.

 Task 2.1

Gather a number of colleagues to discuss the above definitions. Create your own definitions of the terms by using words that will be owned by you and your colleagues.

THE KEY CHALLENGES FOR PERFORMANCE MANAGEMENT

How to involve citizens in measuring performance

Traditional approaches to performance management have not involved citizens and users as widely as they could have. Political support will need to be gained along with managerial commitment to working 'shoulder to shoulder' with citizens in monitoring and measuring our performance. This will be a true measure of local government's integrity in making itself more relevant and exciting to citizens.

Linking individual and team priorities to citizens' expectations

The articulation of a political vision and priorities is now commonplace within local government. However, the real challenge is demonstrating how these priorities truly reflect the aspirations and expectations of citizens. In particular there is a need to reflect how what we have delivered as local government reflects a real social value – our added value.

Commitments to citizens and honest feedback

The community planning exercises of the late 1990s have been a good start in expressing local authorities' commitment to meeting the needs of local people through their involvement in expressing priorities. In some cases strategic priorities and in others operational details are shared by way of targets and outcomes. This new approach to local government of becoming more involving will require a balancing factor – and that factor is honesty. Too often achievable targets have been expressed and then met with great ease.

In recent times all local government would set out priorities with achievable targets, which would be communicated to citizens through the local newspaper or Council paper. More often than not such targets are so achievable that a number of them have been delivered even before they have been communicated to citizens. This is not a cynical view – it is a reality in a small number of authorities. This way of working does not reflect the Council's integrity, values of openness and honesty. Furthermore it does not help to evolve a culture for a high performing, modern local authority. The challenge for new local government is to set ambitious and testing targets reflecting a commitment to improving service quality and performance continuously, achieving best value for citizens. Local authorities that communicate ten targets a year and then the following year take the opportunity in glossy magazines to reflect how they have achieved these targets, do not create a feeling of integrity in the process. Local authorities need to be more honest about setting priorities and tougher targets. Citizens will be much more impressed and have faith in the way we work if we are able to demonstrate that we are trying our best. We must communicate and share with them where we have not achieved our targets and involve them in identifying why this is so, and how such performance gaps can be bridged. In this way we create a relevance for local government and an integrity in the way we do our business.

Addressing the performance gap

There are many ways of identifying performance failure or the lack of achievement at a variety of levels within the Council, in organizations we work with, among teams and among individuals. As local government works more and more closely across sectors and with others, we need to find innovative ways of arguing how to bridge performance gaps. This is particularly relevant where more than one party is responsible for delivering a priority. Not enough attention has been given in the past to the actions and procedures for addressing poor performance, or the performance gap.

Too often, poor performance has attention directed away from it, due to other urgent matters and priorities for the organization. The best value approach will help to address this issue by focusing on the need for continuous improvement. Where there is a performance gap it should be articulated at whatever level and in whichever arena necessary, and new targets set along with time-scales for achievement.

Switching and levering in resources

When a performance gap has been identified at an organization or inter-agency level, a number of routes will be taken to address it. This will require the influencing and negotiation of new targets which may mean a need to contribute more financial, human and other resources in the short term while looking for medium to longer term improvements. The challenge here for local government managers is to understand how to switch resources from other areas and lever in resources to bridge the performance gap.

Switching resources can take place at all levels – operational, corporate and inter-agency. Levering in resources might mean persuading others that they need to contribute resources to help make things happen. A good example here would be to involve the Careers Service and local further education institutions in working with the local education authority to increase take-up of specific bridging courses or career/employment creation schemes. Another example would be for local businesses to contribute financial resources for the expansion of CCTV cameras in a locality to reduce crime and/or the fear of crime.

Developing strategic alliances with other organizations and building relationships can also help to secure funding at national and European levels.

Performance information

The collection of performance data in local government is extremely weak. Some have described it as primitive. There is a need for investment in new financial, management and geographical information systems and online technology to enable managers to measure performance more accurately on a frequent and regular basis at strategic, corporate, operational and neighbourhood levels.

Timely, accurate information can contribute to better and more informed decision making at all levels, inside and outside the organization. New local government will require our organizations to make strategic choices about investment in information and communication technology, to help them in their quest to become high performing, modern local authorities.

CASE STUDY: MANSFIELD DISTRICT COUNCIL'S PERFORMANCE MANAGEMENT SYSTEM

The primary aim of Mansfield's performance management system is to improve performance and motivate employees by concentrating on priority objectives each year, raising commitment, releasing ideas and developing

---

potential. The performance management approach is people- rather than system-dominated.

The primary task of the performance management system in Mansfield is to link organizational requirements to individual performance, ensuring that top level decisions are translated to action at all levels of the authority, making it easier for staff at the front line to pass on suggestions and ideas to decision makers. This is done by cascading corporate and service objectives down to individual jobs. Clarity of process enables feedback to be given from each level upwards through the organization, thus creating a loop for learning.

Supporting the effectiveness of the performance management system is an annual targeted training and development programme related to the priorities of the authority. The programme contributes to improvements in the quality of service management, providing a range of managerial tools and the development of flexible teams and individual skills based on job requirements. Tools and techniques introduced to support the performance management system are:

1. Information technology – provision of critical, timely information to members and managers to support decision making and review of performance.
2. Resource control – uniform systems guided by defined corporate standards to monitor and evaluate service impact and the effective deployment of resources.
3. Benchmarking – annual reviews of service cost, quality and practice through benchmarking with appropriate comparator organizations.
4. Risk management – to assess and minimize all work-related and operational risk, contributing to cost savings.
5. Problem solving process – a uniform approach was introduced which required managers to identify historical and trend data, current deviation from performance, a root cause analysis of the performance problem and recommendations/actions for bridging the performance gap.
6. Management tool kit – team leaders, supervisors, cost centre managers, heads of service and chief officers are required to participate in a learning programme which includes:
   ● an introduction to Mansfield's performance management system;
   ● introducing and maintaining a continuous improvement programme;
   ● benchmarking;
   ● finance for non-financial managers;

> - developing and using critical information systems to enhance:
>   - service performance;
>   - leadership skills and team performance including team briefing;
>   - team and individual appraisal;
>   - coaching and mentoring skills;
>   - risk management and assessment;
> - introduction to and awareness of human resource policies;
> - awareness of grievance, disciplinary and capability procedures.

Mansfield District Council's performance management system, introduced in the mid-1990s, is a good example of a balanced approach to performance management.

REASONS FOR INTRODUCING PERFORMANCE MANAGEMENT

More than ever before in local government coherent approaches to performance management are now needed to help focus on direction and priorities and to reflect best value inside and outside our organizations. There are many reasons for introducing new performance management arrangements; some are described below:

- provides clarity about who is responsible and accountable for ensuring objectives are achieved and with whom, by when, and what the expected outcomes are;
- focuses the organization on priorities, harnessing the organization's energy to those ends;
- provides a balanced approach to monitoring and evaluating performance, learning and feeding back issues to bridge performance gaps;
- clarifies what is expected of individuals, teams and other organizations who are contributing to delivering shared priorities;
- allows feedback to individuals and teams and to citizens and stakeholders;
- creates more openness and honesty about what can and cannot be achieved;
- demonstrates to interested parties that best value is being achieved;
- supports the levering in of resources to maximize the Council's overall performance;
- enables effective use of limited resources;
- identifies performance gaps that need to be remedied;
- encourages learning from the causes of mistakes and successes;
- improves communication inside and outside the Council;

- celebrates achievement, raising staff morale and self-esteem;
- tailors development and training for those who are charged with making things happen.

STAFF DEVELOPMENT AND HOW IT WORKS

Staff development takes a variety of forms and should be treated as an organic rather than mechanistic process. Staff development or staff appraisal (which I believe are part of the same process) are critical elements in a coherent approach to performance management for new local government. The steps in a staff development/appraisal system are set out below. In practice, approaches vary, and the systems adopted are more loose or more formally structured. In many local authorities the term 'performance management' is used to describe a staff development/appraisal system. For clarity I will refer to this element of performance management as 'staff development'.

Reviewing the literature on staff development I can see the confusion that arises due to the variations in terms used. 'Objectives', 'goals' and 'targets' are often used interchangeably for the performance to be achieved; 'appraisal' and 'review' for the assessment of achievement; and 'performance measures', 'indicators' and 'standards' for the measurement and level of performance desired.

Accountabilities:
Identify the purpose for which the job exists; purposes only change as the job changes. Accountabilities should be no more than seven or eight in number. They will describe measurable results and enable assessment of how responsibilities are met.

Objectives (goals):
Objectives will indicate the priorities of a job. They will indicate specific measurable achievements expected over time and they will be based on standards and the accountabilities.

Performance measures and indicators:
These are used to assess achievement of accountabilities and objectives. They will be quantitative and qualitative.

Performance standards:
These are target levels of performance, based on performance measures that are used to set goals and assess achievements.

Action plans:
These will indicate the methods for achieving accountabilities and objectives. They will be used to plan work and monitor progress. They cover assumptions, constraints and deadlines.

Progress review and interim staff development meeting
Progress reviews will occur throughout the performance period, typically of 12 months duration. In the interim the job holder will, with his or her line manager or supervisor, review progress and revised plans as necessary to take on board any new commitments with targets.

Staff development interview:
At the end of the performance period there will be a final review meeting between the line manager, supervisor and jobholder. An overall assessment of achievement of accountabilities and objectives will be undertaken. Performance measures and indicators will be reviewed. This is also an opportunity to identify performance gaps, the reasons for these and therefore the development and training requirements to address the performance gap. Objectives and outline plans for the following year will be constructed.

Staff development and links with other management systems:
The staff development aspect of the local authority's overall approach to performance management will also have some direct and indirect links with a wide range of management systems that are taken into consideration when identifying objectives. They include the following:

- strategic corporate service and departmental plans;
- resource allocation and budgetary control;
- recruitment and retention policies;
- job evaluation;
- salary and grading;
- training and development policy;
- quality issues;
- promotion and succession planning;
- disciplinary and grievance procedures;
- review of personnel records.

Staff development should be linked carefully to the above but not to the extent that it would loose the point of staff development.

Individual staff development has been and will continue to be the method of reviewing performance within organizations. However, as organizations move towards working on an inter-agency basis across sectors and in networked organizations, new ways of appraising performance will need to be identified. This in itself could be the subject of an entire book! We do need to begin thinking through how team appraisal, and in particular 360 degree appraisal, can become more relevant as a way of looking at people's performance in the new local government. Chapter 9 explores more fully the purpose, benefits and application of team and 360 degree appraisal.

Staff development must be introduced with due regard to the impact on other aspects of service and human resource management. The staff development process should not be in conflict with the overall culture the organization is trying to pursue, its priorities and policies.

Staff development of individuals and teams will release and develop their potential, raising their performance by linking their objectives to those of the organization and hence moving towards increasing the authority's performance.

Staff development schemes are developed in consultation with staff and staff representatives. They are kept simple and should link to the overall needs of citizens and, in return, the organization's objectives. They should be used to raise staff morale, recognizing their contribution, developing their skills and abilities to continuously improve the performance of delivering services for citizens.

Where staff undertake duties across teams, functions and agencies, more energy and time needs to be expended in ensuring targets and performance measures are both relevant and accurate.

Preparing for staff development

Line managers/supervisors and the job holder must take the time to prepare thoroughly for the staff development meeting at the end of the year, ensuring that it is a valuable event. At the same time there should be dedicated meetings throughout the performance period to address development needs, recognizing that these are valuable opportunities to seek clarity and gain feedback on performance.

The role of the manager in preparation

Put some time aside to collect relevant documents including:

- job descriptions, notes from previous meetings, action plans and relevant corporate documents such as service and departmental plans;
- external documents with key information, for example area plans, agreements with other external organizations, trends and data to do with the area of service the post holder is involved in. Take the time to draw out key points that are relevant to the job holder's accountabilities and objectives.

The manager should ensure that his or her own appraisal has been undertaken, and targets have been set in order to draw links between his or her objectives and that of the job holder where relevant.

Review the job holder's targets, performance measures, standards and indicators. Look for any constraints on performance, including changes in the environment, that have either helped or hindered the delivery of targets.

Draw together information on the job holder's performance against targets during the past year (use comparative data where you can). Identify what needs to change to help/support the job holder to perform better. Begin to identify new targets for future performance, and consider the development and training required to improve performance both on and off the job (formal and informal).

With the job holder's agreement, the manager should consult the person's peer group, subordinates and others inside and outside the organization where relevant, focusing on how well targets have been achieved and how well the job has been undertaken.

Share key information and conclusions on paper with the job holder prior to the meeting.

The job holder

The job holder should not under-estimate the time that must be put aside in preparing for the staff development meeting – typically around four hours over a two-week period to think through the issues and items for discussion with the manager. Job holders should undertake the following:

- review action plans, targets, performance measures and indicators that were agreed over the past year. Take into consideration any objectives that may have been added. Make notes on how well you have or have not achieved the objectives, with any reasons for performance gaps;
- talk to colleagues, your peer group, subordinates and external organizations that you may be involved with, about how well objectives and targets have been delivered. Use any data available from service users;
- specifically identify issues for over- or under-achievement and the lessons that can be learnt for you and others;
- check whether the performance measures, standards and indicators were relevant and if not why not;
- review the service or operational plan – whichever is the most relevant; identify targets for the coming year;
- list development and training opportunities that should be pursued to help meet performance gaps or improve performance.

At the staff development meeting, performance will clearly be appraised in terms of how well objectives and targets were met. This in itself is very subjective. The following guidelines from Kent County Council are a good example of how performance can be measured against particular grading definitions.

Level 1: exceptional performance
A quite exceptional level of individual performance distinguished by all the accountabilities of the job being developed to the full:

– agreed targets are not only met but consistently exceeded;
– performance is well integrated with the group's/department's/authority's total activities;
– there is continuous drive;
– a confident reaction under pressure and a sureness of approach at all times;
– leadership qualities (demonstrated through staff supervision and/or team work) of a high order are manifest.

Level 2: high performance
A very high level of individual performance exceeding the agreed accountabilities of the job:

– pressure is managed effectively;
– unexpected changes are handled imaginatively;
– agreed targets are exceeded;
– performance is intelligently integrated with the total activities of the wider working group/department/authority;
– leadership (demonstrated through staff supervision and/or team work) and drive are deployed with very good results.

Level 3: good performance
A good level of individual performance where the accountabilities of the job are met in full:

– agreed targets are successfully completed;
– changes in priority are coped with effectively;
– knowledge and skill are applied to good effect;
– flexibility in approach and a willingness to take responsibility are demonstrated.

Level 4: incomplete performance
This category could apply to a member of staff who has failed to achieve objectives through illness or personal problems or who has not yet grown into new responsibilities:

– performance does not reach the required levels;
– some objectives are not met;
– there is a need for the individual to improve performance.

Level 5: unsatisfactory performance
Performance is unsatisfactory with basic requirements of the job not being met:

- the level of output achieved is not acceptable;
- little or no progress is made towards agreed objectives;
- effort is misdirected;
- no imagination is applied to the work.

PERFORMANCE RELATED PAY (PRP)

In the public sector, Marsden and Richardson (1991) have indicated that while managers are not against it in principle, the application of performance related pay often seems flawed. The Sheehey Report into police rewards and responsibilities (1993) included PRP proposals, while recognizing explicitly that pay forms only one element of rewarding performance. In an holistic human resource management system it is recognized that jobs have to be graded first, to ensure basic rates match the scope of the job.

In the LGMB study, *Performance Management and Performance Related Pay* (1994) 14 of the 25 case study authorities operated PRP payments in 1993/4. Two had suspended them for 1993/4 and three had withdrawn them. PRP was generally applied to smaller proportions of staff than performance management. In five case study authorities it extended to over 25 per cent of non-manual workers, but in four it covered less than 10 per cent.

PRP has often been viewed as supporting the performance management scheme, sharpening the way in which it is perceived and underlining its seriousness. A performance management scheme in this context would usually be associated with a staff appraisal scheme related to organizational objectives. On the whole respondents in this particular study felt that their schemes had delivered what was expected in terms of improving individual performance, providing motivation and helping with recruitment and retention problems. PRP has also been introduced as a means of negotiating local pay and is exemplified in organizations that have moved away from national pay and conditions.

Concerns about PRP throughout local government have been raised over the last five years. The principal criticisms are the complexity of local government work (particularly at the more senior levels), the inter-relationships with external agencies which can have a potentially negative impact on the performance of managers, and trade union opposition. A further criticism of PRP is the sheer bureaucracy associated with relatively few targets. Observers have indicated that there is also a risk that PRP could demotivate rather than motivate people: PRP could be divisive especially when it is applied only to more senior staff.

PRP *can* work, but it has potential problems and whether to introduce it or not depends on the views and circumstances in each local authority and the culture they are trying to develop. This sounds like common sense. Unfortunately, too often approaches to performance management are adopted at all levels in the organization without any reference to each other, or worse still they are taken 'off-the-shelf'. In the worst circumstances the tools or techniques adopted may be completely contradictory to the culture and priorities of the Council. A good example here is the Council pursuing team working and developing team priorities and targets on the one hand, and on the other pushing through a bonus scheme based exclusively on individual performance.

Next generation management will be much less concerned with individual PRP, but will be more focused on team and cross-team performance and therefore reward strategies will be more complex and quite often will not involve cash. Some examples of non-cash rewards are:

● direct praise from supervisor, line manager;
● peer recognition in a meeting or a certificate/plaque;
● lunch, dinner or even a drink with the line manager;
● a special award ceremony with invited employees and guests;
● sport or outdoor activities;
● a social function;
● time off to undertake a special project;
● a letter from the very top Council leader, chair of committee or chief executive;
● personal visit from the chief executive, leader or leading member;
● additional development or training opportunity;
● passing on compliments from service users;
● press release;
● photograph with customers or members or chief executive;
● vouchers to purchase learning materials, books or software;
● an opportunity to lead a new project;
● a short secondment or placement to share experience with others.

It is clear that the majority of high performing organizations within local government do not have a PRP scheme. Instead they have a more balanced approach to performance management which incorporates non-cash rewards.

Peter Drucker, creator of the performance concept management by objectives, was heard to observe that: 'MBO is fine, the problem is 95 per cent of the time I don't know what the objectives are'. This may have some resonance for managers in local government. Perkins (1998), responding to the performance related pay initiatives implemented over the past decade or so, adds further weight to the irrelevance of PRP for many. My most positive observation of where PRP has been successful is when individuals employed on short contracts have been brought in to lead and develop change projects. Focused on a limited number of objectives, with the ear of the chief executive and support of a wide range of staff, these external change agents are very successful. Unfortunately quite often they leave behind shattered and demoralized staff as their objectives did not take into account longer term issues and targets for sustaining the change.

In the study carried out by the LGMB, more than 75 per cent of the case study authorities with PRP had assessed its effect on individual performance, 70 per cent its effect on recruitment and retention, and just 50 per cent its effect on clarification of objectives, communications and motivation. The most positive effects were judged to be on recruitment and retention, not performance. Arguments for and against performance related pay, adapted from LACSAB (1990) are:

For	Against
It's fair – it provides a framework for recognizing and rewarding individual's work.	It's unfair – it relies on subjective judgements which can be wrong. It puts the individual before the team.
It motives – encourages people to pursue high standards in the knowledge they will be rewarded.	It demotivates – for those who believe they will never get the extra payments.
It improves understanding between managers and their staff.	It destroys team spirit and can be conspiratorial.
It increases performance and helps to produce a performance culture.	It's distasteful and it complicates managers' jobs.
It helps focus resources in areas where they are most needed.	It's bureaucratic and costly.
It increases control over payroll costs.	It can lead to pay rising faster than performance.

It must be recognized that all pay systems, particularly PRP, become irrelevant over time, particularly in local authorities that are rapidly evolving in the way that they work and meet needs. It is probable that in future new forms of PRP will have evolved that contribute to sustaining different ways of working in new forms of local government.

TESTING YOUR HIGH PERFORMING CULTURE

Here is a self-assessment questionnaire. Once you've completed it and totted up your score, you will be able to assess how much of a high performing culture exists within your work area.

For each of these questions score 0, 1, 2 or 3 as follows:

0 – totally disagree with the statement,
1 – there is some semblance of truth in this statement,
2 – there is a lot of commonality between this statement and what happens in my work area;
3 – this is how it is in my own organization.

- Staff are committed to each other, willing to pitch in, coach and support one another to do whatever tasks are necessary to get a job completed.
- I am empowered to make decisions on operational matters within existing guidelines.
- I am empowered to make decisions on operational matters outside service guidelines.
- When things go wrong the emphasis is on what can be learnt and how we should work differently, not who is to blame.
- When something is done very well, time is taken to understand the causes of that success so that the learning can be shared.
- New ideas are welcomed and positively encouraged. Time is taken to assess the possible impacts on service results.
- Managers reflect behaviours consistent with the Council's values. The Council's vision and values are discussed, and staff understand how their jobs fit in to the overall direction of the Council's work.
- Staff are able to ask without fear why particular decisions have been made.
- Front-line staff as well as managers elsewhere in the service demonstrate leadership to support the vision, values and priorities of the Council.
- Staff accept responsibility for the results of their work; they demonstrate a high level of commitment to successfully completing actions and care about the outcomes.
- Team working exists to a high degree within the service and across the Council, inside and outside.
- Individual differences and the contribution of team members are respected.
- The service plan for your area is a key determinant of your own objectives and priorities.

- You meet regularly with your line manager/supervisor to review progress.
- Your line manager takes seriously the commitment and responsibility of developing you as an individual and team member.
- You spend time formally and informally with your manager/supervisor who coaches you on your performance, and reinforces good performance.
- You are encouraged to identify your own development and training opportunities to help develop your abilities and improve overall performance as both an individual and a team member.
- Teams, individuals and ways of working are regularly challenged in terms of what value they add to the work of the service.
- Line managers, supervisors and staff focus much of their work on positive developments, best practice and good ways of working.
- Formal structures and processes, manuals and guidelines produced by the organization do not inhibit creative thinking within your team.
- You feel valued as a member of staff by your team members, line manager and supervisor.
- There is good communication between your team and the other teams you work with and in particular the other service areas that work closely with your service. Each team understands the priorities and needs of the other.

What your score means

0–19: Seek help! Question seriously whether you are making a contribution to the overall direction and business of your organization. People know you exist, but what do you do? How are you valued? Why does the organization need you?

20–29: Much of what you do does not reflect a high performing culture. Why is this so? What benefits can you gain from moving towards a high performing culture? Take steps to review entirely your performance management systems and how they relate to individuals, teams and the organizations you work with, and the priorities of the people you serve.

30–39: Managers and staff support traits of the high performing culture, but there are some serious gaps in how you work as a team or in terms of relationships with one another. Take some time out to discuss what these gaps are and how you can address them.

40–49: You reflect all of the traits of a high performing culture. There may be some small gaps in how you work. Do you know what they are? How can you address them? Well done, you are probably doing a good job and are valued by the people that work with and for you.

50–59: Well done; you have all the traits of a high performing culture. Think about how you can harness individual and team commitment further to add value to what you do. How can you sustain this way of working?

60–66: Why not share your secrets with others?

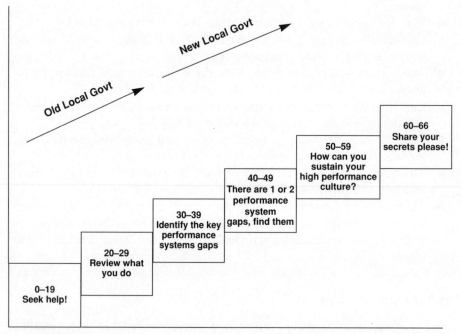

Figure 2.1 *Testing your high performing culture – the scoring staircase*

SUMMARY

This chapter has helped to pull together contemporary thinking about performance management, what it means, the key terms and definitions. The link between individual performance, PRP and good staff development has been explored. The questionnaire for assessing performance management culture is a simple and subjective approach. In Chapter 3 a more holistic framework is presented, covering all dimensions of performance management.

REFERENCES

Fogarty, M (1998) *Performance Management: Terms and Conditions*, LGMN, London.

LACSAB (1990) *Handbook on Performance Related Pay*, LACSAB, London.

LGMB (1994) *Performance Management and Performance Related Pay Survey*, LGMB, London.

Marsden, D and Richardson, R (1991) *Does Performance Related Pay Motivate?*, London School of Economics, London.

Perkins, J (1998) *Successful Performance Managers Ask the Right Questions – Human Resources Guidance and Practice in the Public Sector*, IMS, London.

Sheehey, P (1993) *Inquiring into Public Responsibilities and Rewards*, The Stationery Office, Norwich.

3 A framework for leading-edge managers

Having considered in Chapter 1 the new local government context and next generation management, and in Chapter 2 contemporary approaches to performance management and the challenges for the future, you will have concluded that approaches from the mid-1990s on performance management are inappropriate as they stand. Although many authors have written about the need to link aspects of strategy to the approach to performance management, few have made or indeed offer a coherent and holistic approach.

Performance management in terms of next generation management concerns making the links across all levels of organizations using techniques that span all of performance management. Managers in local government who want to stay ahead of the game despite the limited resources available to them, know that they need to clearly understand a number of issues. They need to understand much more widely and in greater depth:

- who the users of their services are;
- who the potential users are;
- the competition in the market for delivering the same service;
- the combination of alternative delivery mechanisms that they can adopt to improve performance.

Leading-edge managers will be associated with next generation management. Such managers will develop their ability to learn from processes they are involved in, so they own them and continually apply them to new circumstances. They will learn how to use and adopt new tools and techniques from different sectors and ways of working that can help improve performance at all levels. Leading-edge managers will continually question what they do, monitor, evaluate, reinvent and find different delivery mechanisms for meeting the needs of citizens directly and indirectly. They are learning managers.

Alternative delivery mechanisms, whether they are trusts, joint ventures or contracted services, will all test managers' and elected members' ingenuity in ensuring that these arrangements are accountable to citizens in terms of their performance and probity.

This chapter sets out a new performance management framework for leading-edge managers. Guidance is given on how best to use it as a diagnostic tool, avoiding barriers to change, and suggestions for how best to develop your strategy for a high performing local authority are discussed.

LEADING-EDGE MANAGERS IN LOCAL GOVERNMENT

Managers reading this book will be doing so for a number of reasons. They will range from those wanting to develop and gain knowledge on how best to approach the implementation of performance management in the new local government, to those seeking new solutions for old problems and, just as importantly, those wanting to make a difference in their own management capability and performance. How can we therefore differentiate old managers from leading-edge managers? Talk to any number of managers in your local authority and the chances are that nine times out of ten you will be talking to an old style manager. New local government managers are as I have termed them leading-edge managers, who will demonstrate a range of characteristics. These characteristics are described in the following paragraphs.

Social justice, quality and good government

Leading-edge managers will have a high level of commitment to and understanding of the values of social justice, quality and good government.

It is possible that many managers currently working in local government and within agencies supporting local government make a significant contribution to the performance of their organization. However, they may not necessarily have a high level of commitment to the values of social justice, quality services and good government. One may question whether a commitment to such values is necessary. I have from time to time come across managers who neither understand nor have a commitment to such values. Thank goodness they are in the minority! At the same time a number of these managers can be seen to be making a significant contribution to the performance of their organizations. Why is it then that leading-edge managers of the new local government will need to display these characteristics? New local government is arguing that local government is about more than the public administration of services and enabling and facilitating services for citizens. New local government argues that we have a significant role in terms of civic leadership and governance for our localities and hence the need to build new relationships with our citizens who at the same time are our customers. It is for these very reasons that leading-edge managers will need a deep and inner understanding of the values we talk about here, as it is their behaviours, the culture that they evolve around their work environments within and outside the Council, that will influence how new local government is perceived by citizens.

Capacity to learn

An exceptional capacity to learn through listening, doing, research, education and self-development will be a trademark of leading-edge managers.

Leading-edge managers are able to learn through different styles and in different ways. They will of course have preferred styles, but to capitalize on their environment and learning opportunities they will learn continuously through listening to the people they serve – citizens, service users and potential service users, the people that work with them and for them. SK Chakraborty of the Indian Institute of Management has coined the phrase 'brainstilling', which he says comes before the process of brainstorming. Brainstilling as Chakraborty describes it is about taking stock and listening to what others have to say and contribute. This is an appropriate term for new local government.

Learning from best practice alone is not enough, as best practice is often described in terms of what has been done well, yet fails to distinguish and point out the differing circumstances others operate in. Therefore managers need to be able to process their learning through doing as well as reading. This will mean constantly evaluating and questioning the appropriateness of how they and others are applying themselves. Leading-edge managers will need to invest time in researching their area of service. Just as any private sector organization needs to invest in research and development, so does the individual manager. Education by way of accredited learning courses through universities and business centres can appear to be a luxury for many managers in local government in times when there are pressures on resources and people. However, leading-edge managers will undertake more than one form of accredited education during their careers.

There is a desperate need for a 'world class' qualification for public sector managers. The old Master of Public Administration programmes are no longer relevant as they mostly interpret in very crude terms what is taught on the Master of Business Administration courses. As we have discussed in earlier chapters, local government and the public sector around the world have changed significantly. The issues we face are similar although our circumstances are different. There is a need to rewrite entirely what public management in the new millennium is about. Indeed, in my experience of working in South Africa, Russia and Japan, all the indications are that governments are looking for international learning which can be transcribed into a world class programme for leading-edge managers. I believe that this will be a reality imminently. Outward-looking learning Councils will provide placement opportunities not only within their organization but within other sectors in other countries too. The secondment scheme with the Cabinet Office and the shoulder-to-shoulder international exchange placement of local government officers between UK local authorities are good examples of next generation management development activities.

Self-development techniques such as neuro-linguistic programming (NLP) and transactional learning (see Chapter 9) will become more important for individual managers as a part of their fundamental portfolio of learning activities.

Understanding new tools and techniques

Leading-edge managers will need to have their eye constantly on the ever-evolving approaches to improving organizational, inter-agency, individual and team performance. As local government and its environment change, so too will the need to apply new tools and techniques and ways of working. Individual performance appraisal will be replaced by 360 degree appraisal; strategic plans will be replaced with community inter-agency and area plans; performance reviews will be replaced by inter-agency scrutiny panels. Soft partnerships will be replaced by strategic alliances to meet higher levels of performance requirements and lever in resources over a longer period of time.

Wide networking

Leading-edge managers will be entrepreneurial in their approach to organizing services through their propensity to continuously network inside and outside their organizations, sharing and gaining knowledge of new and better ways of carrying out their business or delivering their services. More specifically, in the future leading-edge managers will:

- understand and thrive on information and communication technology to do their work;
- establish and work in flexible work teams inside and outside their organizations, both as leaders and as subordinate members to achieve operational and higher level goals;
- spend time thinking about how better to relate their business to the needs of current and potential service users, thereby becoming more innovative and taking calculated risks.

Leading-edge managers in the future can, and will, work at all levels within an organization's strategic, corporate and operational functions. As organizations become smaller and more multi-task-oriented, managers will need to be like chameleons in the way they approach their work at different levels inside and outside the Council.

Task 3.1

How well do you measure up against this competency profile for leading-edge managers? Are the gaps concentrated in any particular area or are they spread out fairly equally? Consider what you need and how you might develop these competencies.

THE NEW PERFORMANCE MANAGEMENT FRAMEWORK

Why a new framework?

The new local government environment differs greatly from how local government has operated over the last 20 years. Contemporary frameworks and systems do not help us apply the required organic approach to performance management for new local government. In fact the new local government environment is so complex that its inter-relationships (see Figure 1.1) with the state, market and civil society and in turn their relationships to the strategic, corporate and operational arenas in local government, mean that we need to have a 'calculus' approach. By this I mean an approach that is not systematic but is organic, and different for every Council based on its local circumstances, its political, social and economic environment. It is on this assumption that the new performance management framework has been designed.

The new performance management framework is not a definitive or a static framework. It is a map that local government managers can use to diagnose where they are currently focusing their energies, resources and processes to achieve high performance, and it is also a framework for mapping out a journey to achieve high performance and modernization for the new local government. The framework is shown in Table 3.1.

The new performance management framework is not as awesome as it may at first appear. Let me take you through it. There are four key quadrants, each with a primary heading describing an area of performance management relevant to the new local government.

Quadrant 1: civic leadership and democracy

This quadrant is about new local government and its relationship with citizens as customers. It is about local government's role in involving stakeholders, citizens and other agencies. It is about the role of members and political accountability and the rights of citizens.

Table 3.1   *The new performance management framework*

A NEW PERFORMANCE MANAGEMENT FRAMEWORK

CIVIC LEADERSHIP AND DEMOCRACY

Citizens and Performance	Political Management	Macro Performance	Information and Measuring Performance
		STATEGIC PLANNING	
Consultation strategy	Scrutiny of policy	Performance plans	Performance measurement
Citizens panel		Service planning	Performance indicators
Area working	Community plans	Strategic foresight	Market intelligence
Best value	Vision	Partnerships	
Commitments and guarantees	Member performance	Alternative delivery mechanisms	Benchmarking
		Resource switching	Networking/family comparators

RESULTS-ORIENTED PEOPLE   **OPERATIONAL CONTROL**

Organizational Performance	Individual and Team Performance	Quality Standards	Operational Frameworks
Investor in people	360° appraisal	Quality assurance BSI/ISO	Audit
Business excellence framework	Mentoring/ coaching	TQM	Statutory inspections eg, OFSTED, SSI
Core competencies	NLP/TAL	Financial and HR procedures	CCT/VCT
Development and training plans	Employee involvement	CRE standard	Zero based budgeting
Learning organization	Virtual teams	Service chain analysis	

Quadrant 2: strategic planning

This quadrant is about the connectiveness between short, medium and long term planning, the links to citizens' needs and expectations. It is about how local government plans the use of its resources and how it influences the use of resources from other agencies to make things happen for citizens. Just as importantly this quadrant is about how information is obtained, used and made available to plan services and to measure the performance of service delivery, and about how information is used to make decisions for the future of our localities, what is and is not needed. In strategic management terms this quadrant is about understanding the performance requirement of the organization.

Quadrant 3: Results-oriented people

This quadrant is about how people as both individuals and teams work together to deliver the performance requirements of the organization. It is about developing the capability of organizations, individuals and teams.

Quadrant 4: operational control

The fourth quadrant of this framework is about systems and processes that ensure specific standards – an essential element of local government in terms of checks and balances. This quadrant is also about how ways of working can influence performance and the quality of the services delivered by the organization.

As you begin to read through the tools and techniques and ways of working described in each of these quadrants, you will begin to build a picture of how your own local authority relates to the new performance management framework. As mentioned earlier, these approaches do not constitute a definitive list; rather they are ways of working that can be associated with next generation management. Although one can add further tools and techniques in each of these quadrants, I caution you against adding ways of working associated with old local government as this will lead to styles and a culture that are not relevant. Rather than helping us to move forward, they would hold us back!

Each of the quadrants is further segmented into two arenas. These arenas are important clusters of activity. They help us to understand, in a more focused way, the arenas in which our local authorities are expending energies. They also help us to understand where we are not directing energy and therefore highlight areas that need to be addressed. From this you begin to see the framework providing a valuable diagnostic tool.

Citizens and performance

This arena focuses more closely on how local authorities plan to involve citizens and service users in setting service priorities and measuring performance. The arena is about new ways of involving citizens on a face-to-face basis with both managers and elected members. There is a plethora of new approaches to community participation, including citizens juries, citizens panels, community councils and area reference groups. These are described in more detail in Chapter 5.

Political management

Over recent years this term has increasingly been used to describe the relationship between the strategic and political management of local authorities, how members work and perform their roles and responsibilities inside and outside the Council. In this arena political management is about how citizens, stakeholders and other agencies are involved in the scrutiny of policy put forward by elected members. It concerns how elected members have engaged the organization in working with the community and stakeholders to develop vision and values culminating in area and community plans that are owned across their localities and not only by the Council itself.

Macro performance

In another decade this arena of activity might have been called 'strategic management'. However, I think we need to be more explicit here. Performance in this arena is at the macro level and is about the overall performance of the local authority, the planning of that performance and the targets associated with other agencies, stakeholders and citizens. Macro performance is also about how existing resources are used and switched around the Council and other agencies to deliver citizens' priorities.

Macro performance for next generation management will include strategic foresight. Strategic foresight is about planning for the future, taking into consideration known facts, givens and information, to ensure that those futures are not just possibilities, but will indeed happen. Strategic foresight will be about making futures happen through strategic alliances, through the absorption of knowledge and accurate information about the environments in which we operate, social and economic factors, how markets operate, and what citizens' needs are. The near future is predictable. Leading-edge managers will undoubtedly apply strategic thinking tools and techniques to help them come to the most probable scenarios.

Information and measuring performance

This is closely allied to the previous arena. If macro performance is about strategic foresight based on information, then how well we undertake the activities within this arena to provide timely, accurate and relevant information is critical not only to macro performance but also to the overall performance management system of the local authority. This arena of activity is also about testing the quality of our work and performance against the performance of others. In some instances like-with-like comparisons of service areas will be made. On other occasions aspects of a service, for example the management of the Social Services inspectorate, could be benchmarked against the management of the quality control function of a health trust. This arena of activity is also about the alignment of information inside and outside our organization, and how we communicate with others in terms of our performance.

Organizational performance

This arena of activity specifically focuses on approaches to developing the capability of organizations and areas of service. It is about the style and philosophy that the organization is pursuing to improve its overall performance, linked into all other aspects of the organization's work and culture. The achievement of the Investors in People award or the European Foundation for Quality Management's Business Excellence Framework award are not the ultimate goals in transforming our organizations to high performance. As Nelson Mandela put it, it is the process of transformation rather than the output that is most important. My own experience has been that approaches such as the Business Excellence Framework have helped organizations to go through the thinking process in terms of analysing how they work and continuously measuring this against agreed standards and targets. This leads to a culture of continuous improvement and high performance endemic within the organizational structures and processes, and of course the behaviours of the people that work within the organization. The question of how to involve us in cross-service or indeed inter-agency teams is more difficult here. A manager working in one team may be using the Investors in People concept and standard, yet in another organization he or she could be pursuing an alternative quality assurance system or standard. This remains a challenge for leading-edge managers.

Individual and team performance

This arena of activity is about the way in which teams and individuals work and how their objectives and priorities are linked to the needs of citizens and organizational priorities. It is also about how the performance of individuals and teams is assessed and how they are supported to develop to deliver the performance required. There is absolutely no doubt that the future structure of local authorities will not be departmental or directorate-based. Instead it will be based around clusters of cross-functional and networked teams. The use of virtual teams (ie, a group of individuals who are brought together to undertake a task or provide a function for a limited period, or indeed on a permanent basis, while having other tasks and responsibilities) is a distinct possibility in different parts of local government in the future. Once this becomes the case, it will be increasingly difficult to justify performance appraisal schemes for individuals.

The propensity must be towards a more inter-agency approach to monitoring and evaluating performance. A key implication is that there will be a level of managers whose job it will be to move around virtual and cross-functional teams inside and outside the Council, discussing how well performance targets have been met, what the performance gaps are and what the resolutions should be for meeting them. These will not be inter-agency police officers; they are the future advocates for citizens.

Quality standards

This arena of activity is about systems and procedures for ensuring specific standards of service. It is also about how well processes are analysed to ensure high performance and how standards to do with social value, in particular equality between gender, race, etc are part of the overall formula. The Commission for Racial Equality's standard is a good example of a singular focused approach in the delivery of local authority services. The use of this standard is admirable. However, aspects of the standard are possibly better translated into a local authority's overall approach and integrated into its approach to Investors in People or indeed the Business Excellence Framework. Approaches to ensuring quality standards can be bureaucratic and static. New local government requires optimum flexibility and creativity to ensure that resources are moved and targets are altered as and when needs change. Here lies a dilemma for leading-edge managers.

I once had the opportunity to speak with Sir John Harvey Jones, former chairman of ICI. He tells a wonderful story of when he became chairman and announced that all manuals, including personnel manuals, should be thrown away in line with the then current management thinking. He was then overwhelmed by a barrage of ad hoc, meaningless, divisive approaches to managing and making decisions on personnel matters. A valuable lesson was learnt: although an organization should not be entirely driven by bureaucratic manuals and procedures, there is a place for agreed principles or ground rules. In local government, particularly for purposes of probity, accountability, equality and fairness, agreed principles and ground rules for how we work are important.

Operational frameworks

This arena of activities is to do with internal and external control frameworks for ensuring that standards are adhered to, whether they are financial, to do with service delivery or legislative requirements on processes for competitive tendering. Operational frameworks in this arena are also about the ways of working which are self-imposed by local government to ensure a desired outcome. Good examples of this include zero-based budgeting and voluntary competitive tendering.

THE FRAMEWORK AS A DIAGNOSTIC TOOL

Stage 1: 'brainstilling'

Use the process of 'brainstilling' to understand what currently happens within your own organization in terms of performance management. Remember 'brainstilling' is a process of listening to the views of others and pulling this information together. During the 'brainstilling' process you should be consulting colleagues inside and outside the organization, elected members and service users. There may be data available to you from previous activities to help you understand what currently happens within the organization. Prior to beginning the 'brainstilling' activity you must decide whether you are undertaking a diagnosis of your service area, or of your whole organization. It is quite possible to undertake this diagnosis several times over to reflect the differences between what happens within your own service area and what happens generally across the Council.

Stage 2: evaluate information

How well does your organization undertake and use the tools, techniques and approaches you have identified? What is the level of political and managerial commitment to these ways of working? Were they forced upon you or did they evolve through searching for new and better ways of measuring and understanding performance? This evaluation of the information you have collected will help you to make a much more qualitative judgement for the next stages of the diagnosis. It may be helpful to undertake this particular stage within the team environment, taking on board the views of a range of people to help achieve a more balanced view.

Stage 3: rating commitment and ownership

Following the evaluation stage you should have some fairly informed judgements about the level of understanding and the degree of seriousness with which the tools, techniques and approaches in the new performance management framework are regarded within your organization.

Working through each of the eight arenas systematically, beginning with citizens and performance, take each activity and give it a rating in terms of commitment, ownership and how the tool or technique is valued:

1 = not used
2 = used, but there is no commitment or ownership
3 = there is neither a negative nor a positive view
4 = a fairly positive commitment and ownership

5 = a very high and positive commitment and ownership; it is valued by both managers and citizens

6 = exceptional commitment to this way of working; there would be great dissatisfaction among managers, staff members and/or citizens if we withdrew it.

Depending on how many people you would like to involve in this process, other approaches could include a short questionnaire circulated to a wide range of individuals inside and outside the Council to weigh commitment, ownership and value of the tools and techniques and approaches. Some of the approaches will be unfamiliar to citizens and would require some explanation.

Also consider how the questionnaire in Chapter 2 on testing your high performing culture could be used to supplement the diagnostic approach in this chapter.

Stage 4: chart your status

Drawing together the information from stage 3 you should now be able to chart the status of performance management within your organization for each of the eight arenas in the new performance management framework. Use each of the axes in Figure 3.1 to plot your result and then join the points together. You will see a picture emerging of where your organization concentrates its efforts in terms of its approaches to performance management, and more importantly the level of commitment and ownership and how these approaches are valued.

Stage 5: questioning

In which arenas or quadrants is your authority strong, in terms of its approaches to performance management? How does it measure up against the culture of the organization? Does it support it or is it in conflict with it?

What kind of culture is being supported within your organization as a result of the way in which you approach performance management, for example is your approach balanced across the different arenas and quadrants or is it particularly focused in one area?

Stage 6: envisioning

You have now come to some further conclusions about the strengths and weaknesses of your local authority's approach to performance management. It may be balanced across the quadrants or it may be skewed in one arena or quadrant, giving rise to implications for the other arenas.

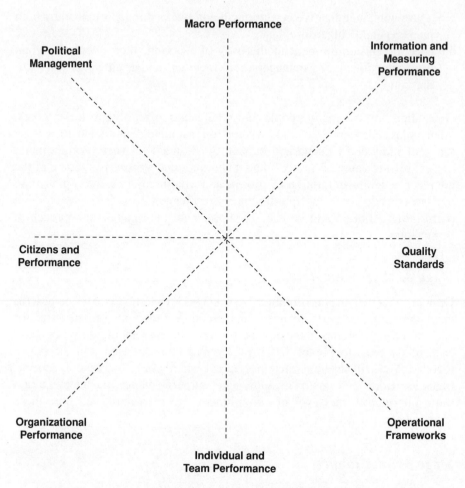

Figure 3.1 *New performance management framework diagnostic chart*

Stage 6 is not so much a diagnosis, rather a process for envisioning or looking forward to where one would like the organization to be – in this context the organizational culture one is trying to create. Using Figure 3.1, how much further up or down the axes would you like to move the authority in terms of your balanced performance management approach? Now draw a dotted line between each of these points joining up the axes (see Figure 3.4 for a completed example). Once again a new picture emerges indicating the direction you wish to pursue in terms of developing your performance management culture.

The new performance management framework can be used as a simple diagnostic tool. The accuracy of the diagnosis depends on the amount of time and the involvement of others that is invested in the six stages.

As previously indicated the arenas do not reflect a definitive range of approaches, tools and techniques. It is possible for you to insert additional ones in your framework. However, I once again caution against using outdated ways of working that are no longer relevant for new local government or indeed next generation management. Including such approaches will serve only to dilute the messages emerging from the diagnosis.

MAKING CHANGES AND MOVING FORWARD

Moving forward to pursue the organization culture of a high performing, modern local authority will require a robust approach to the management of change within your organization, particularly if the gap between where you are now and where you want to be in the future is significant. The purpose of this section is to help you think through some of the potential barriers to change, and how to sustain your desired approach.

Intermittently I have been a great fan of The Industrial Society. Over recent years they have produced some very good illustrations and approaches for management. Figure 3.2 illustrates the steps to considering change. I think it is incredibly useful for managers to think through how best to move forward on the next steps to developing a high performance culture.

STRATEGY WORKS BACKWARDS

Pedler *et al* (1991), in their book *The Learning Company*, use the illustration of a strategic staircase to describe how one can develop a strategy. I will use this simple principle to help you think through your strategy for developing a high performance organization. It is important that we accept the fact that you can only work out a strategy by going backwards from where you want to be, not from where you are. Use Figure 3.3 to think through the key steps in creating your strategy for moving forward.

Step 1: what culture are you trying to create for your local authority (eg, high performing, modern local authority)? You have already diagnosed what the organization culture is now. Identify a time-frame for when you want to achieve your strategy. Working backwards down the stairs, ask yourself what are the other key milestones for steps 2, 3 and 4? Step 4 will take you back to the bottom of the stairs, which is where you are now.

This procedure may appear to be simplistic, but I have used it with many groups for helping to develop strategies for moving organizations forward. In practice, you will move up and down the staircase as you figure out what the key milestones are. Don't worry. You can of course create slightly more steps, but be aware you may only lengthen the change process.

MANAGING THE COMPLEXITY OF CHANGE

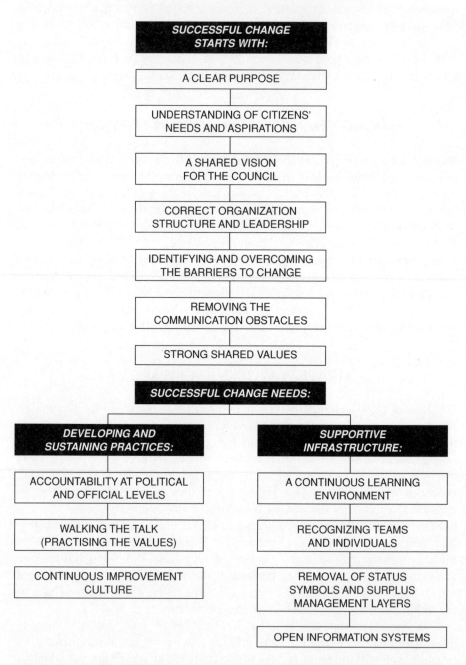

Figure 3.2 *Managing the complexity of change (adapted from The Industrial Society)*

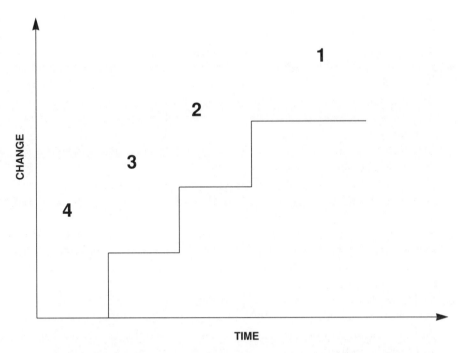

Figure 3.3 *The strategic staircase (adapted from Pedler et al, 1991)*

Why change fails

Local government has experienced an unprecedented amount of internal and external change, largely as a result of changes in society and technological advances all impacting on 'how and what' people expect from local authorities. Many of the lessons are documented in a wide range of reports, articles and books. The following is a summary of some of the pitfalls, of how and why change fails. Please do try and avoid them in your journey to creating a high performing, modern local authority.

- Quick fix option or fad – limited or short bursts of energy devoted to a new way of working, or a new approach supported by one-off management seminars; worse still, posters, tee-shirts and even coffee mugs. A key message from the leader and/or chief executive at the beginning of the change process and nothing more.
- Previous change – your organization may well have embarked upon a wide range of initiatives over recent years. Some will have been rather more successful than others. People in your organization and outside your local authority will be aware of success or otherwise of these approaches.

Previous approaches may give others ammunition to prevent or impede your current endeavours.

● Misunderstandings about change – change will inevitably involve different ways of working; it is not a single activity or event.

● Poor communication – how often have we heard of the need for a good communication strategy or action plan? It is definitely true that where communication issues are not thought through carefully or where information is given in an ad hoc way, the grapevine will take over, with disastrous consequences.

● Key milestones over long periods – planning change over a long period does not necessarily mean that we avoid looking for short term goals and targets. Sharing (with staff) the longer term targets alone is not helpful; people need to see benefits, successes and key milestones achieved quickly. These are important.

● Tunnel vision – members and management may suffer from tunnel vision, looking only at the end result and not taking into consideration the implications for other aspects of the local authority's work or, most importantly, how citizens will respond.

● Vision and values – these are important aspects for next generation management organizations. Without these, people have no real sense of purpose and direction. Where they exist they should be reflected in the way that the individuals, teams and elected members work.

● Inadequate monitoring – there may be a clear strategy with key actions over a period of the change programme. However, failure to monitor implementation regularly (and learn from the experience) and poor information systems are not helpful.

● Organizational and staff capability – too often local authorities expect managers and staff to undertake changes and new ways of working without recognizing that our people are not suitably equipped to work in new ways and that our organizational arrangements contradict what we are asking them to do.

● Competing activities – a complaint of almost every manager in local government: competing priorities distracting and diverting the focus on key change management initiatives. We need to dedicate resources to sustaining and leading the change initiative.

A survey reported in *The Economist* in 1992 found a number of barriers to quality, ranked according to how many times they were mentioned by managers. The results are shown in Table 3.2. Although this survey was undertaken within organizations in the private sector, there are some incredible similarities to local authorities and we can learn some of the lessons and issues on which we should focus attention.

Table 3.2   *Survey by* The Economist *(1992)*

Issues	Percentage seeing this as a barrier
Top management commitment	92
Too narrow an understanding of quality	38
Horizontal boundaries: functions and specialisms	31
Vested interest	29
Organizational politics	28
Cynicism	28
Organizational structure	27
Customer expectations	26
Speed of corporate action	14

The performance management system in Mansfield District Council was used as a case study in Chapter 2. Figure 3.4 illustrates where they are currently in terms of their approach to performance management. The dotted line indicates how they would like to re-balance their approach. The lines drawn around the framework can be described as the performance management calculus for Mansfield District Council. As such it is about the relationship between ratios and differentials. In the performance management framework the ratios are the tools and techniques used in the arenas and the differentials will be the local circumstances and environment of each and every local authority.

In effect the re-balancing of the Council's approach to performance management is their journey to achieving 'high performance and modernization'.

SUMMARY

In this chapter we have developed the profile of a leading-edge manager for new local government. In parallel to this the use of a new performance management framework was introduced, enabling a more coherent and holistic approach. The framework is a powerful diagnostic tool for understanding the current and future performance management culture desired. Each of the arenas of activity within the four quadrants of the framework is

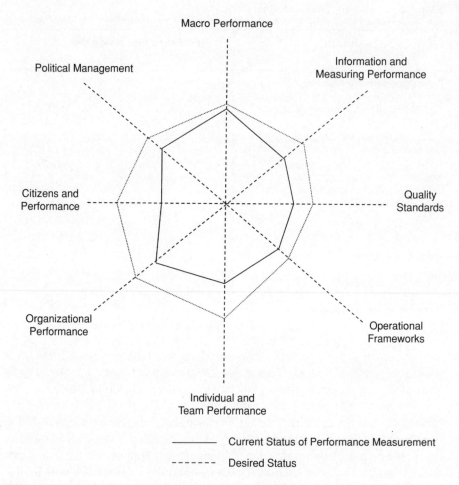

Figure 3.4 *The new performance management framework – diagnostic chart for Mansfield District Council*

considered in the following chapters, along with tools and techniques, case studies, checklists and best practice.

Chapter 4 explores in more detail the contribution of the political and strategic management arenas of this framework to improving performance.

REFERENCE

Pedler, J, Burgoyne, J and Boydell, J (1991) *The Learning Company – A strategy for sustainable development*, McGraw-Hill, Maidenhead.

4 The political and strategic management contribution

What is the political and strategic management contribution to ensuring performance management? Both councillors and officers have critical roles to play in ensuring that new local government is active in all arenas of the new performance management framework. Only by such a thorough involvement can they hope to create the culture necessary for a high performing, modern local authority.

This chapter will explore what we mean by political management and strategic management, the interface between how elected members do their work and the strategic management role of chief officers and senior managers. This constructs the context within which middle managers concerned with performance management work.

WHAT IS POLITICAL MANAGEMENT?

Political management concerns the roles and responsibilities of elected members, and how they work and discharge their civic leadership role as the only democratically elected people within a locality. It concerns the interface between a Council's political organization and the officer organization.

It also concerns the relationship between elected members and officers in facilitating a vision for their localities, influencing and negotiating resources inside and outside the Council, to ensure that citizens' needs, priorities and expectations are met.

There are over 20 000 local councillors in the UK. Each plays a vital role as the elected representative of their local community. Councillors in the UK are charged with ensuring the efficient and effective use of over £40 billion of public money. They provide the core relationship of the industry of local government – the representative democracy for local people. However, as we have discussed in earlier chapters, local government is in need of revitalization and a part of this process is the transformation to new local government.

I have worked with leading councillors in several authorities for over a decade. My experience and research tells me that there are a few major obstacles preventing councillors from becoming more effective in carrying out their roles and responsibilities. They include a huge amount of time spent in unproductive committee meetings focused on detailed operational issues, and the lack of development and support offered for undertaking their roles and responsibilities. Allied to this are personal issues to do with time. It is not only the wide range of committees that take up time, but a plethora of informal and formal Council member working groups and parties. The study carried out by Professor Ken Young on behalf of the Local Government Management Board, *A Portrait of Change* (1997), clearly indicates that the roles and interests of elected members are changing and this will have implications for relations with officers.

The informalization of decision making processes indicates that authorities are still experimenting with different ways of working in terms of their committee arrangements; this is shown in Table 4.1.

Young's report is incredibly helpful in highlighting members' roles, the barriers to be overcome and the tasks and skills involved. I have chosen to reflect on this particular illustration as it helps us to see some of the similarities and differences in terms of skills and abilities of members and for leading-edge managers. The illustration is taken from a report for the LGMB by Steve Leach, Lawrence Pratchett, David Wilson and Melvin Wingfield at De Montfort University.

STRATEGIC MANAGEMENT

The objective of strategic management is to identify and understand what is really important in the context of a Council's vision and political direction, and to effect necessary and appropriate change in the way a Council is managed. This in turn impacts upon what business is undertaken and how it is carried out. The intention is ultimately to make a positive difference for citizens.

Professor John Stewart has described strategic management as 'changing an organization to enable it to meet changing needs and to express changing values'. Tom Peters has described it as 'involving the implementation of an explicit plan that has captured the commitment of the people who must execute it; that is consistent with the values, benefits and culture of these people; and for which they have the required competence to deliver'.

There are many more definitions of strategic management; what is important is that there is an agreed definition within your organization.

Table 4.1 *New roles of cultural barriers and skill implications (from Leach et al, 1997)*

New role emphasis	Cultural barriers to be overcome	New member tasks and skills involved
Policy scrutiny	Why should we open up our policies to public scrutiny and criticism by backbenchers and/or opposition members?	• Well briefed and phrased questions – and the skill of probing questioning of witnesses. • Diplomacy skills – asking searching questions in a way which doesn't alienate external witnesses.
Strategy formulation	Isn't that what the leadership groups should be doing? I'm primarily a local representative and strategy has little relevance to my role.	• Working in a different, more open relationship with officers (two-way informal questioning). • Brainstorming, lateral thinking, problem solving. • Strategic analysis – seeing the strategic issue in the mass of detail.
External networking	Many of these bodies have responsibilities which should be ours (and/or are quangos). External networking is the officer's job.	• Understanding aims and interests of other agencies. • Negotiating/bargaining skills (based on clarity of perception of our purpose). • Identifying areas of common interest.
Community development	Why do we need community participation when (i) we've been democratically elected on the basis of a manifesto; (ii) I've been democratically elected to represent this ward.	• Two-way advocate – representing views of local community to the Council and representing views of Council to local community (including why it can't be done). • Spotting gaps in representation of local interests. • Finding the right format for stimulating debate.

Strategic responsibilities

The term 'strategic' can be used to describe responsibilities at all levels within the Council.

The strategic roles and responsibilities of the 'top team' – chief officers group or board – is about more than providing a framework within which resources can be systematically planned in order to achieve specified objectives within a set period of time (strategic planning). The strategic responsibilities are about the process by which the Council looks beyond the requirements of existing services to the changing environment, working closely with the political leadership to identify key:

- issues for communities;
- policy changes required;
- priority areas for protection and/or growth and resource switching;
- organization and management changes required to realize strategies;
- strategies for alignment and integration; and
- performance management issues to realize the vision.

Top management's strategic responsibilities include:

- Strategic leadership: the capacity to give direction to the organization and to maintain the momentum.
- Strategic organizational development: developing the Council's capacity to achieve its purpose and to meet environmental change.
- Strategic thinking: identifying the important among the apparently routine; distinguishing the highly valued in a conflict of values; working out the policy/organizational change that will have maximum impact with minimum disturbance. Seeing the incompatible between problem and policy or between policy and organization; seeing how opportunities for change can be created.

Top management's strategic responsibilities can be summarized as:

- Setting the direction needed to achieve the Council's vision.
- Establishing clear values and principles to be shared throughout the organization.
- Overseeing the working of the Council to ensure that it is directed at achieving the vision and political priorities set by the political leadership.
- Ensuring the Council has the necessary resources to implement decisions. This includes ensuring that managers are equipped with the support they need and are given clear priorities.

Directors and executive directors

A wide range of current research findings clearly indicate the move towards more streamlined management structures within local authorities. Allied to these is the emergence of strategic directors and the executive and corporate director role. An LGMB survey of internal organizational change data shows that 31 per cent of authorities abandoned departments for directors between 1989 and 1992 and a further 13 per cent between 1992 and 1994. The main purpose of these strategic director roles has been to form an executive board, with the chief executive or a strategic management team which is hands-off from the day-to-day responsibility of operational services. However, each of the strategic directors still has performance management responsibilities for a cluster of services which may change from time to time depending upon a variety of factors such as government legislation and development opportunities for other colleagues.

There is mixed evidence about the success of these changes. What is clear is that as with most changes in the strategic management of local government their success or failure depends upon clarity in the way in which members respond to the new arrangements. Unless members realize that the day-to-day operational management of the Council is not a matter for them, any system of officer management will be undermined by the expectation that it will provide a conduit for members to interfere in that routine work.

Experience from the early to mid-1990s has helped authorities to evolve a new definition of the strategic director. The most popular title currently in use is 'executive director'. The roles and responsibilities here include strategic thinking, strategic and organizational change, change management, strategic intervention, corporate performance management, and external relations.

The need for leadership in strategic management

Next generation managers in local government will need real leadership as a key characteristic. Dr Trevor Bentley (1998) provides us with a number of pointers as to what real leadership is and how it is seen and experienced:

- Real leaders are people who others want to follow.
- Real leaders are people who don't want or need the limelight and who give credit where it is due.
- Real leaders are servants to those who follow them, making sure they are well fed, protected and able to see in the dark.
- Real leaders exercise their power by giving others authority.
- Real leaders never blame anyone except themselves when things go wrong.
- Real leaders know that they are successful because their followers are successful.
- Real leaders know that they need to unconditionally love and support their followers.

Task 4.1

How does your boss compare to the above statements?

There has been an interesting development in the debate about leadership that is particularly important for next generation management. It is to do with transactional leadership and transformational leadership. Transactional leadership can be seen to relate more specifically to competencies (management) for which there is evidence that can be developed. Transformational leadership dimensions are typically referred to as 'qualities, attitudes or personal predispositions' (Alimo-Metcalfe, 1998). Kotter's (1990) comparison of transactional and transformational leadership, shown in Table 4.2, may be helpful here.

Table 4.2 *Kotter's (1990) comparison of transactional and transformational leadership*

	Transactional Leadership (Management)	Transformational Leadership (Leadership)
Creating agenda	Planning and budgeting: developing a plan – a detailed map of how to achieve the results	Establishing direction – a vision which describes a future state along with a strategy
Developing HR	Organizing and staffing: which individual best fits each job and what parts of the plan best fit each individual	Aligning people – a major communication challenge getting people to understand and believe the vision
Execution	Controlling and problem solving: monitoring results; identifying deviations from the plan and solving the 'problems'	Motivating and inspiring: satisfying basic human needs for achievement, belonging, recognition, self-esteem, a sense of control
Outcomes	Produces degree of predictability and order	Produces changes – often to dramatic degree

The debate is about whether or not one can develop managers with predominantly transactional competencies to adopt a transformational orientation as well. I believe that this is not only possible but essential if true leadership is to occur across new local government at the strategic and operational levels.

Task 4.2

Consider whether you are a transactional or transformational leader. If you are a transactional leader how easy do you think it will be to become a transformational one?

VISION AND DIRECTION

A key role of political and strategic management is to help facilitate and foster the development of a vision. More than ever before, new local government will require a clear vision that is communicated and shared both inside and outside the Council by staff and citizens and by those that live and work in their localities. A vision will provide direction and a sense of purpose and will enable local authorities to harness their energies and resources to meeting that vision. New local government will link vision for the locality to performance plans, neighbourhood plans, and service plans right down to team operational plans and individual performance targets.

Figure 4.1 shows a nest of plans linking a local authority's plans together. Notice the connection of all the plans in the core of the nest. The leading-edge manager must understand the connectedness of these different plans. The nest of plans is a good illustration of how mega, macro, meso and micro plans should be linked.

Any organization, public or private, should have a set of team, section, department and corporate plans. These plans must ensure that every member of staff can 'see themselves' within each part of the organization and how their part links up with the overall approach. However, a local authority needs to achieve more than that. It must link each of those plans with a vision that is shared by citizens. Here are two different ways in which local authorities have involved the public in creating their 'vision'.

CASE STUDY: VISIONING CONFERENCE

North Hertfordshire (Hitchin) and Hertfordshire District Council held a joint two-day visioning conference. It was open to local residents and businesses and representatives of organizations and agencies. The conference was called to develop principles to guide the preparation of a strategy for the area. The conference led to an agreed set of objectives for development of the town and priority actions, and the establishment of seven action planning groups (which continue to meet) to develop their ideas, and a series of specialized focus groups covering the interests of young people, the unemployed, disabled groups, business tautology and ethnic minority groups.

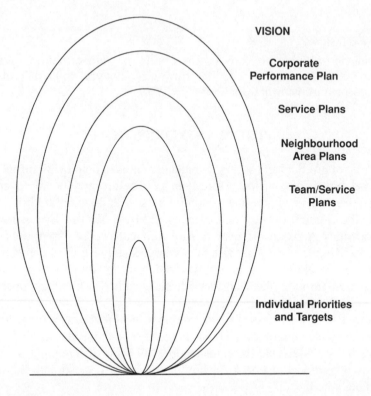

VISION

Corporate
Performance Plan

Service Plans

Neighbourhood
Area Plans

Team/Service
Plans

Individual Priorities
and Targets

Figure 4.1 *The nest of plans linking vision through to individual performance*

CASE STUDY: 'CHOICES FOR BRISTOL'

Another good example of working with communities to create vision was 'Choices for Bristol'. In March 1996 'Choices for Bristol' published a discussion guide and up to 7000 copies were distributed through the Bristol evening newspaper.

Between March and October 1996 ideas were collected from groups who had used the guide and through roadshows held at public focal points such as libraries, health centres and supermarkets. More than 2000 ideas on how to improve the city were generated. In December 1996 two 'Vision Bristol' meetings were held for adults and young people to turn ideas into achievable goals. There were more than 300 participants. Six vision statements were produced describing the anticipated goals for the following years. In February 1997 statements and ideas were published as 'Your Ideal Bristol? Lets Make it Happen', and individuals and groups were invited to join action groups.

'Choices for Bristol' and the Hitchin and Hertfordshire District Councils' approach to involving others in creating visions are just two of many examples of new local government. Members are working with officers to plan events that involve citizens and enable them to put forward their ideas, taking them on board with great integrity, then communicating them back outwards in a much wider way so that performance can be measured.

Setting performance at a neighbourhood level

Localities are one of the core elements of the industry of local government. Every local authority has a geographical boundary. Beyond that line they have no responsibilities; within it a great deal. Over recent years local authorities have been using localities within their boundaries to organize a different relationship with their public. Since the 1980s there has been a growing number of local authorities devolving powers and decentralizing services to area and neighbourhood levels. There has been a great deal of experience, some good and some incredibly bad. A number of Councils have tried to decentralize entire departments; others have taken a more evolutionary approach in decentralizing parts of services over longer periods of time.

New local government must build on these experiences, looking towards working politically and managerially at a neighbourhood level. This may not work everywhere but it does provide a way of helping coordinate services at a local level. It also provides a basis for inter-agency working and building relationships with local people, listening to their needs and concerns. In the context of next generation management, working at the neighbourhood level will mean involving citizens in establishing performance indicators and monitoring and evaluating performance at a local level.

In terms of the local governance agenda, neighbourhood or area working would provide a mechanism for involving citizens in local decision making on policy matters and even in the scrutiny of important local issues. If a local authority has decentralized within its boundaries, it provides the leading-edge manager with the opportunity to develop in each locality a relationship with the political management structure which will add an important dimension to their performance management.

There is a wealth of experience of working at a neighbourhood level; some is shared below.

COMMUNITY ACTION FORUMS – SOUTHAMPTON

The community forums are controlled by local people. Each forum is an autonomous body whose inaugural members set the constitution. Most forums include individual residents, while some have a membership made up entirely of representatives of local organizations.

All forums have at least two types of meeting: large open meetings and small planning meetings which usually consist of a committee of elected members who organize forum meetings and run forum business. While councillors are welcome at all large meetings, this is not always the case with committee meetings. Some committees may allow councillors to attend the small planning meetings, where they may be allowed to vote; others do not allow any councillor participation. Their main function is to advise the Council on issues of local concern.

COMMUNITY PLANS

Community plans are the product of community-wide consultation between local authorities, citizens and stakeholders across localities. Community plans express the vision and commitment of elected members working closely with officers, to facilitate others in the community to express and share their views which can then be integrated into an overall plan. Community plans form an integral part of the strategic management and planning process of a Council and therefore act as a bridge between the political management and the strategic management of the Council. Members have a role in helping to facilitate the creation of a community plan through their civic leadership. Managers have a role in terms of their involvement in the planning systems of the authority, and in redirecting and organizing the authority to work in different ways to meet these expectations.

Quite often meeting these expectations in the new local government context will mean further cross-service and inter-agency working, adding to the complexity of the relationships between all of those involved. When a local authority tries to publish what it hopes to achieve for local people in a community plan, we begin to see the complexity of the relationships and the networks inside and outside our organizations. We realize the importance of a vision, direction, clarity of purpose, shared values, and ownership of processes, as critical elements of next generation management. It is here, through people and the integrity of their behaviours and the values that they espouse, that organizations and communities can be helped to make the right links.

I once attended a lecture by Professor Mark Swilling of the School of Public Management and Development at Witts University in Johannesburg. He told how the apartheid regime in South Africa was challenged and eventually broken down and replaced. He described it as a process of evolution where hundreds of thousands of individuals were involved in tens of thousands of meetings over many years, talking about a vision of a non-racial South Africa and values of equality and access. They talked about these things in their workplaces, in their homes, in their communities. Professor Swilling went on to describe this as the process of movement that eventually bought down the apartheid regime. This is a powerful analogy of the need to share values, as these will create a common denominator, helping people to move in the same direction, working on the same goals. Just as a set of shared values can bring down a regime, so it can bolster an organization.

The following two case studies are good examples of how local authorities have looked outwards, shared values and created visions. Together with their communities they have translated them into priorities and targets and have begun the process of involving others in monitoring the achievement of their performance.

CASE STUDY: DEVELOPING A RELATIONSHIP BETWEEN THE COMMUNITY AND A NEW UNITARY COUNCIL

BRIGHTON AND HOVE COUNCIL

Brighton and Hove Council is a new unitary authority. It was formed in April 1997 out of two towns that had long but different histories of consultation with their communities.

Advisory panels

The Council wanted to harness local energy and enthusiasm and to do so took the step of establishing five advisory panels which would enable members and other interested individuals and agencies to look at a range of key issues and then advise the Council of their findings. This approach meant members could work alongside community representatives and others to gain a clearer understanding of:

- council services;
- strategic issues;
- how to engage others;
- how to work in partnership.

The five panels were:

Early years
Health
Older people
Quality of life
Youth.

Each flexible agenda allowed them to focus on issues which were of particular local concern. For instance, at only its second meeting, the health panel highlighted the challenge the towns faced in respect of suicide, mental illness and substance abuse. It then based much of its subsequent work on looking at ways to take those ideas forward in the Council. It was important not to compromise services by placing additional burdens on them at a time when they were having to grapple with post-reorganization transition.

Community planning and citizens' research

Having established the panels, the Council wanted to take the opportunity to involve the community in its planning and budget making processes. It chose to do that through community planning.

The community planning process involved the Council in sending a short, readable booklet to every household in the towns, outlining some basic information about services and asking people's views on five pledges designed to tackle key issues such as jobs, crime, environment and what made Brighton and Hove and their local area special.

The citizens' research, originally intended for 1998, was pulled forward a year so as to provide a statistically valid framework into which the community planning findings and advisory panel feedback could be fitted.

Both pieces of work were undertaken quickly, so that the results could inform members in shaping service plans and budgets for the forthcoming year. Equally important, it was recognized that added value would only be gained if members were able to read across the different pieces of information and get insight as to what that meant for them as ward councillors. A special member community planning group was established as a working party of the performance quality and accountability sub-committee, which oversaw the whole process. Using census and other data the members themselves began to use the information to highlight local issues and ask more searching questions.

The consultation and research has helped the Council to be confident that when it asks its citizens: 'What should be our priorities?', 'How well are we performing?', 'How can we improve?', it will enter into an informed debate by starting such a dialogue in an open and honest way. The local authority can win and build on the trust, confidence and qualities of its different communities. It will now be taken forward through the Council's approach to best value, confident in the knowledge that when the Council genuinely involves its communities it can expect fair and informed feedback which strengthens and deepens the ties between members and those who elect them.

CASE STUDY: CITIZENS AND STAKEHOLDERS SETTING AND MONITORING STRATEGIC PRIORITIES

COVENTRY CITY COUNCIL

Coventry City Council has always had a pretty robust approach to planning the best use of resources to meet policies and priorities. And, as one would expect within a climate of ever-decreasing resources, the approach has been largely finance-driven which, in so far as it goes, has served the Council well in terms of proactive management. In recent years the Council has become policy-driven and put a lot more effort into involving the community and key stakeholders in the setting of policy priorities. The Council has taken the driving seat in developing many strategic and operational partnerships, and the 'partnership approach' has become an established and accepted means of delivering effective services.

In 1997 the Council began community planning in earnest. The intention was to involve the community fully in both setting the policy priorities for the city and also in holding the relevant people and organizations accountable for their performance. The Coventry Community Plan is a bit different, as it is a plan for the city as a whole and not just for the services of the Council.

The Council acted as the facilitator and enabler in bringing together all the key stakeholders for the city. This included contributors from all the main public agencies and also from other sectors – health, police, education, chamber of commerce, public–private partnerships, the voluntary sector, large and small businesses, community organizations, charitable organizations, etc.

Over a period of about nine months a common set of agreed priorities for the city was finalized: more jobs; tackle crime; tackle poverty; invest in young people; create an exciting, vibrant city centre; and meet the needs and aspirations of older people.

The work was intense and the consultation far-reaching. There were two city conferences held, each of which gathered together about 120 of the city's leaders, movers and shakers. Elected members held their own mini-consultation conferences in their electoral wards and the whole thing was supported by media campaigns, posters, leaflets, telephone hotlines, competitions, questionnaires, etc.

With a huge commitment and ownership of the seven priorities the focus turned to actually making it happen – putting the theory into practice.

To oversee the process a City Forum was established. This is a voluntary organization that meets about four times a year, and is made up of about 25 key strategic leaders from across the city. The City Forum's initial task was to set up Programme Delivery Groups (PDGs) – one for each of the priorities. The PDGs are made up of key players from each of the relevant organizations for each priority. They are people who can exercise a 'power of influence' over their own organization in terms of commitment and resources.

Each of the PDGs was charged with developing a fully resourced, owned, action programme to deliver the priorities of the Coventry community plan. The action programme had to set out clear targets, leadership, timescales, responsibilities and resource identification. These targets have now formed a set of locally meaningful performance indicators which will be published. These indicators act as the performance measures of success and each PDG will be held accountable by the City Forum which in turn is accountable to the people of the city. How local accountability works for the Coventry Community Plan is shown in Figure 4.2.

The City Forum reports to the public twice a year to demonstrate progress on the priorities, and over time the public will be able to monitor and evaluate progress. The City Forum reports through the local media and

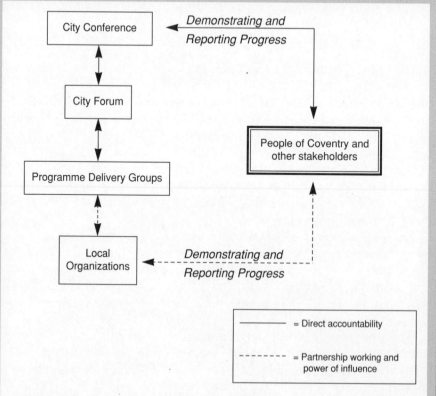

Figure 4.2   *Local accountability through the Coventry Community Plan*

direct to the organizations involved. In addition a city conference is planned every other year to ensure that the long term priorities of the Coventry Community Plan remain timely and appropriate to the real needs of the city.

The Coventry Community Plan was officially launched in February 1998 and already there are early signs of success. The local authority has undertaken a significant resource-switching exercise to redirect its resources to the seven priorities, and its political management structures now reflect the priorities of the plan. There are also indications that other key partners are taking similar steps with the planning of their resources.

Coventry's Community Plan may not be perfect. But it is a good example of how new local government can engage citizens in setting strategic priorities and operational targets, and link them to the plans of relevant agencies within the area.

SCRUTINY

'Scrutiny' is a term that has emerged in the late 1990s as a key word associated with the agenda of modernization and is freely used by both members and officers. However, I believe that there is a lack of understanding of what we mean by it. 'Scrutiny' is described in *The Oxford English Dictionary* as 'critical gaze, close investigation, official examination of ballot papers'. Unfortunately – or fortunately as the case may be – the most frequent use of the term in local government has been in connection with ballot papers. However, there is some very good experience, particularly associated with citizen juries, which has involved the scrutiny of key issues and policy matters.

The model that some local authorities have developed for their 'scrutiny panels' has been taken from the select committee system of the House of Commons. This committee system was developed in the 1980s to provide the House with an opportunity to scrutinize in detail areas of policy that were either being discussed as a possible way forward or had already been implemented. The membership of select committees reflects the political complexion of the House of Commons, but never contains any ministers. In this way they genuinely represent an approach that is external to the government, with some real independence. Over the years, especially when the government has had a large majority, select committees have represented one of the main ways in which the government has been held to account.

In the early 1990s a number of local authorities set up a similar system of committees, although these were usually called 'scrutiny committees'. They contained representatives from both political parties and had only backbenchers on them. They have been developed in two ways: first, to scrutinize policies and practices external to the local authority, such as the health service or the local water company; second, to scrutinize local authority services. It is almost certain that this form of political management will grow.

In the context of the new performance management framework, I believe that scrutiny, as a key role of members, should involve critical examination of policy before it is implemented, and also the scrutiny of performance at an authority or city-wide level.

However, when scrutiny panels are used, they provide an important part of the performance management system of a local authority. Leading-edge managers concerned with performance management should recognize that their own system of performance management must interact with whatever political system of performance management exists within their Council.

CASE STUDY: PUBLIC SCRUTINY

LONDON BOROUGH OF HARINGEY

Haringey has introduced a procedure called 'public scrutiny'. Topics are identified from opinion surveys or other sources. A public scrutiny meeting is held in the Council chamber. This is attended by a range of individuals including service providers, representatives of service users and members of the public drawn from interested users, voluntary organizations and residents associations, a public scrutiny panel of councillors and in some cases an outside expert.

Service users' representatives are invited to sound out opinion from service users and present their findings at the scrutiny meeting. They raise issues, make suggestions and ask questions. They are asked to complete a public scrutiny submission document setting out their views and questions to assist the panel's preparations. The panel of councillors also asks questions of the service providers. The service providers make a presentation at the meeting about the service, the standard set and future plans. Regular follow-up reviews are undertaken to monitor the Council's progress in responding to the issues raised.

The process is intended to help the Council to:

- increase direct contact between service users, councillors and service providers;
- foster working relations between councillors and managers in constructively improving the quality of services;
- assist in ensuring that future service standards reflect the issues raised at the public scrutiny meetings.

(Source: LGA, 1998)

LONDON BOROUGH OF SUTTON

A slightly more traditional (yet just as effective) approach to scrutiny is the London Borough of Sutton's scrutiny working party. In 1997 the Council established a scrutiny working party of elected members reporting to the policy sub-committee of the policy and resources committee. The working party is responsible for a system of service scrutinies covering priority areas identified through monitoring performance against the Citizen's Charter performance indicators, and spending comparisons in relation to 'family' authorities. The scrutinies involve in-depth analysis of cost and performance data and interviews with relevant managers to analyse service delivery processes. Findings are reported back to service committees for action, which is monitored on an ongoing basis.

(Source: LGA, 1998).

SUMMARY

In this chapter we have begun to unpack some of the complex interrelationships between political and strategic management, leadership and the contribution of citizens. Members and officers have a crucial role to play in ensuring that mechanisms exist at a corporate and city-wide level to engage citizens in terms of their contributions to developing a vision and direction for our localities.

In Chapter 5 we begin to examine in more detail how to engage citizens through a wide range of consultation mechanisms, both to set targets and to monitor performance.

REFERENCES

Alimo-Metcalfe, B (1998) *Effective Leadership*, LGMB, London.
Bentley, T (1998) 'CEOs who get in the way', *Management Services Journal*, May, pp 20–55.
Kotter, J (1990) *Force for Change*, Free Press, New York.
Leach, S, Prachett, L, Wilson, D and Wingfield, M (1997) *All You Need is Trust? The Changing Relationship Between Members and Officers*, LGMB, London.
LGA (1998) *Democratic Practice: A guide*, LGA, London.
Young, K (1997) *A Portrait of Change*, LGMB, London.

5 | Citizens and performance

There is a general acceptance that to reinvigorate local government there will need to be a significant focus on the development of its civic leadership role. This must lead to development of approaches to public participation, involving citizens in articulating and prioritizing their needs, hopes and fears at a local and city/town-wide level. Furthermore, citizens will need to be inspired to judge how well local government has facilitated, influenced and negotiated on their behalf to meet their needs, expectations and priorities. In this way local government begins to nurture new relationships with its citizens who are also its customers, ensuring integrity in the way it works.

New local government is about sharing power and becoming more accountable.

Leading-edge managers in new local government will analyse the plethora of approaches for creating public involvement. Those involved in performance management, in setting performance targets and priorities and in monitoring will be particularly concerned at how local people can become involved in these activities. The implication here for leading-edge managers is that you will need to understand more clearly the methods that are available, the purpose of each of them, the advantages and disadvantages, and the appropriateness of using them for your local circumstances. The involvement of managers with citizens is an important aspect of developing a performance culture; it is as important as the publics involvement in performance management. Consultation and involvement are not ends in themselves, but a vital part of an holistic approach for new local government.

This chapter begins to explore the many different ways of involving citizens. It builds on case study material I have collected over the last few years as well as from a wide range of organizations including the Local Government Management Board (LGMB) and Local Government Association (LGA). There are important implications for leading-edge managers regarding their development and training requirements in these areas, a topic that is dealt with by way of a case study later on in the chapter.

Involving citizens is qualitatively different from collecting information or even consultation. We must begin to make a distinction between the consumerist and democratic approaches. The dilemma for local government is that we are now beginning to see the citizen also as a consumer but the essence of local government is that the consumer must be involved as a citizen. Therefore local government's approach to its customers must be democratic. Involvement must be about having a say in services and having opportunities to have a wider say on how services are produced and delivered, and how they impact on individuals and our wider community.

In involving citizens in the governance of their localities and in identifying needs and priorities, we will require local authorities to make decisions on the most appropriate method to use.

Participation is about involving people in decisions rather than asking them what they think or expecting them to decide. However, this does not mean that citizens take decisions just because we have an open approach to participation. In practice there is not a clear boundary between consultation and participation.

CASE STUDY: GOOD PRACTICE GUIDE ON PARTICIPATION
SANDWELL METROPOLITAN BOROUGH COUNCIL

Participation is:

- empowering
- inclusive
- long term
- time-consuming
- open
- hard work.

Participation is not:

- tokenism
- exclusive
- one-off
- quick
- secretive
- easy.

New local government has a growing interest in democratic innovation and public participation. It is underpinned by the determination to enhance the civic leadership role of local government. It aims for greater participation in annual elections and encouragement to experiment with new models of political leadership.

Consultation strategy

Consultation should not be haphazard. It must be part of an overall approach to the public. New local government needs to react openly to feedback from those they serve. At the same time they must have a clear strategy for how to encourage public participation. Leading-edge managers will understand that in their overall business and service plans they will need to incorporate the consultation strategy that links into local services they are responsible for. This approach must also link in with the overall approach of the local authority to citizen involvement in setting priorities, and monitoring and evaluating performance.

Very few local authorities have comprehensive consultation strategies. Where they exist they are not culturally integrated into the whole organization's approach to service delivery and therefore miss out on the benefits of learning from the involvement of citizens.

The modernization agenda for local government (DETR, 1998) outlines four broad messages for involving citizens:

1. Seeking the views of the citizens – these approaches enable local authorities to introduce lay experience and views into their decision making. They include current and informed views.
2. Recognizing communities by increasing their involvement in direct decision making – the need to recognize the differences between communities of place and communities of interest and ways in which they can be involved formally and informally in decision making at an operational and policy level.
3. Watchdog or scrutiny role – direct involvement of citizens in scrutinizing policy before and after implementation, scrutinizing and monitoring performance before and after delivery.
4. Opening up Councils – changing the role of individual citizens in formal structures of local authorities including co-options onto committees and public question times at Council meetings.

The first two of these four points will be discussed in this chapter.

SEEKING THE VIEWS OF CITIZENS

There is a range of techniques to be used here. They need to be broken into two categories: seeking the current view of citizens and seeking the informed view of citizens. The current view provides a snap-shot of public opinion in so far as it exists at any one point in time. This view does not depend on the public necessarily being briefed or informed about all of the facts or issues.

The snap-shot recognizes that citizens have a democratic right to a point of view whether they 'know all the facts' or not.

Opinion polling

Opinion polling will allow you to obtain a broad representative view on an area of service, and elicit specific responses. Some opinion polls, usually those carried out around election times, are trying to find a 'representative sample' so the poll will tell you what the whole population thinks. Other polls do not seek to be representative. Polls will allow you to evaluate the experience of service users and use the information as a basis of future changes. Opinion polls can also gauge all sorts of opinions about services which the respondents have never experienced and know little about.

Opinion polling can be carried out through door-step interviews, street interviews, or circulating questionnaires for self-completion. Some local authorities have encouraged communities to undertake some of these activities themselves.

CASE STUDY: OPINION METERS

SOUTH LANARKSHIRE

Opinion meters are an adaptation of information technology to opinion polling. In South Lanarkshire there are electronic meters, or recording devices, set up in shopping centres and other places the public frequent. Customers, visitors and passers-by can use the meters to record their opinion on questions posed.

This is an excellent example of information technology being used to seek the views of service users on the performance of the Council. Other opinion polling techniques that could be adopted to obtain the views of service users and citizens include polling booths in shopping and leisure centres, telephone polling and household questionnaires.

Survey techniques

Surveys can be used to evaluate experience and build up profiles of service users and communities and to assess comparative needs. They can also assess the quality of performance in service delivery. The techniques used will differ from opinion polling as they aim to provide a wider perspective on issues and are particularly suited to seeking group or community views.

Mystery customer survey

This is a popular technique within the service sector and over recent years has become even more popular in specific service areas in local government. It is a market research technique which helps to evaluate the experience of service users who contact local authorities by telephone or in person. The following case study can help us understand this particular technique more clearly.

CASE STUDY: MYSTERY SHOPPERS

HAMMERSMITH AND FULHAM CONSORTIUM APPROACH

Three London boroughs led by Hammersmith and Fulham employed four mystery shoppers who played the part of customers seeking information about a service. A set of 50 frequently asked questions were agreed among the authorities, covering all areas of service, including equalities. Each mystery shopper made 50 calls and asked 50 set questions. Over a three-week period over 6000 calls were made. The ability of the authorities to provide written information was also tested.

This multi-authority approach was specifically used to compare performance on a key corporate area of service delivery with other best value-minded local authorities. It was used to measure best value in specific services as part of their performance review processes. The most important aspects of this approach are the need to establish that the right questions are being asked and that the mystery shoppers are familiar with the local authority structures so they understand the processes and the responses received.

Priority search

A survey method I have helped to develop over the last ten years is priority search. Priority search involves the application of specialized numerical methods to qualitative data, allowing surveys to be carried out that can capture the richness and detail typical of structured individual interviews but in a fraction of the time and at a fraction of the cost.

The priority search begins by defining an open question which sets the boundaries of the research to be carried out. This may be very broad, for example 'How can the Council improve services for you?', or a tightly focused question, such as 'What needs to be done to improve the refuse collection service?' Following this, a small but reasonably representative number of respondents are invited to respond, either individually or in focus groups. The result of this process is a set of ideas which as far as possible cover the whole agenda of the target population. The 'bottom-up' nature of this process makes it extremely sensitive to issues that are current for those who are consulted.

Next, a questionnaire using a sophisticated paired comparison technique allows respondents to prioritize a substantial set (30 to 40) of these responses. Detailed management information is then produced by linking individuals' priorities with biographical or demographic information obtained elsewhere on the questionnaire. It is possible to examine in detail the wishes, hopes or expectations of any sub-group of the population surveyed. The software used automatically calculates levels of statistical significance and all the charts generated display this information as an integral part of the output.

Priority search is an excellent tool that is extremely malleable in terms of the settings and environments it can be used in.

Representative panels

The purpose of representative panels is to obtain regular means of representative polling to track the views of service users over a period of time, and for more effective and focused opinion poll development. Putting together panels of people can be another method of obtaining opinions or attitudes of a representative group. Panels differ from surveys or opinion polling in that they are usually constituted on a standing basis so that a similar group of people are consulted regularly. This provides a useful device for tracking opinion over time.

CASE STUDY: THE SOMERSET STANDING HEALTH PANEL

A standing panel has been used by Somerset Health Commission. In the mid-1990s eight health panels were set up each consisting of 12 people as a representative sample of the population. Their brief was to discuss the values that should guide health resource allocation decisions. Panels held four meetings over the following year.

The first meeting brought out the panel members' own health issues and at succeeding meetings they discussed issues raised by the district health authority or by the family health service agency. After discussion, members completed a series of decision sheets which were then added up. A facilitator prepared a report for the health authority, using discussions to convey the flavour of the panel meetings as well as the results from the decision sheets.

Panels are on-going and four members are replaced at each meeting. Unlike citizens juries, standing citizens panels lack quality of deliberation, but do give back valuable information.

Citizens panels on a town- or city-wide basis can also be helpful for a Council in researching the views of citizens on its performance. Bradford Metropolitan Council has a panel of 2500 citizens, put together in conjunction with Bradford Health and Training and Enterprise Council. It assists these agencies in identifying individual views on a wide range of issues including service performance over time.

SEEKING INFORMED VIEWS ON PERFORMANCE FROM CITIZENS

Citizens juries are perhaps the most interesting and valuable way of getting informed opinions on our performance in service areas from citizens, as they go beyond a 'snap-shot' of opinion. The Institute of Public Policy and Research was the first organization to carry out research into citizens juries and pioneered the idea in practice in the UK.

What is a citizens jury?

Citizens juries are a way of involving the public and the community in local authority decision making processes and reviewing performance on city-wide issues, priorities and targets. They are a structured approach to obtaining citizens' views on issues of importance. Citizens juries are not just about hearing evidence from a range of witnesses: they can also be about calling agencies or elected members and officers from within service areas to give evidence about performance and service quality. This is clearly a challenging use of the citizens jury approach.

Members of the jury have the opportunity to examine issues in depth, to learn about the workings of the local authority, and make real contributions to public affairs. A typical citizens jury would be made up of between 12 and 16 people, selected as far as possible to be representative of the community, with a balanced mix of gender, age and ethnicity, employed and unemployed people.

In many cases the topic under discussion will be a controversial one on which opinions are divided. For this reason the citizens jury approach to monitoring and evaluating performance is especially suitable as it enables a rigorous debate and discussion about what has and has not happened, what was promised and what has been achieved.

Meetings are spread over four days, with the jury hearing presentations from witnesses giving different sides of the argument. Some of the presentations would be from local authority officers, others from professionals and representatives of other agencies' managers and staff responsible for the area of service. There would be an independent moderator to help the jury process run smoothly, and the jury would have its own advocate or 'jurors' friend' to assist the questioning and discussion. After debate, the jury would draw up its conclusions in a report to be presented to the Council.

Compared with other models, citizens juries offer a unique combination of information, time, scrutiny, deliberation and independence. The conclusions of citizens juries are not necessarily taken on board by local authorities or indeed other agencies. However, they are an important contribution in terms of opinion and independent evaluation on performance and will inevitably influence decisions made by elected members and officers.

It is difficult to calculate the cost of running a citizens jury process. Clearly it will vary according to the amount of time required during the process and in the preparation stages and the attendant research. Issues such as whether jurors are paid, witnesses' expenses, accommodation, etc need to be taken into account. Estimates for a four-day jury range between £16 000 and £20 000.

CASE STUDY: CITIZENS JURIES, SOUTH LANARKSHIRE COUNCIL

South Lanarkshire has run two citizens juries and was one of the first Councils to do so. The first had an urban focus: the Hill House housing estate and the issue of graffiti and vandalism. The second had a rural focus, considering the issues of providing services for older people in such areas. In both cases topics were selected by residents using a variety of research techniques.

The Council made it clear to both citizen juries that it would not necessarily undertake to implement all of their recommendations, but gave its full undertaking and commitment that recommendations would be seriously discussed and, where possible, implemented. The reasons for not doing so would also be made public. The recommendations of the first jury, focusing on Hill House, have been well progressed.

South Lanarkshire Council members do not believe that this way of working was necessarily better than other approaches to community participation. They recognize the importance of choosing the right method for local circumstances. They concluded that the use of citizens juries aided and informed the decision making process, and that this method should be complemented by other techniques.

CONSULTATION GOOD PRACTICE NOTES FOR MANAGERS

The interpretation of a local authority's consultation strategy, its depth and integrity, will quite often depend on political commitment, managerial enthusiasm for wanting to understand better our service users and markets, and of course the expertise within the organization to develop both corporate and local approaches.

Here are seven tips to ensure good practice in consultation, taken from Rawson (1997):

1. Be clear about why you are consulting and what change is possible and let people know.
2. Plan the consultation with reference to all others who have an interest, including elected members of the Council.
3. Be clear about who is the target for the consultation and use a method(s) which suits the needs of the target group(s).
4. Know what you are going to do with what you find out.
5. Let people know if and when problems arise.
6. Follow up the consultation quickly with effective action.
7. Publicize the time-scale for responding to findings and let citizens know what is happening and link actions to your performance/or service plans.

The consultation checklist shown in Table 5.1 is a development of these tips. You may find it helpful to use this checklist with your team when looking at how to improve the service quality and performance of your area of activity. It is important to recognize that many of the services we provide or enable are undertaken on a cross-service and inter-agency basis. For this reason the preparation for consultation must include the involvement of other agencies and services that are responsible for producing and delivering the service.

Table 5.1 *Consultation checklist*

Knowing why you are consulting, what change is possible and letting people know it
Why
What do you want from the consultation?
Why are you doing it?
How will you use the information you get?
Change
What change is possible?
What principles are underlying the consultation?
Letting people know
Who needs to know what your position is?
How will you communicate with them?
What will you tell them about how they can influence the outcome?
Planning the consultation with reference to others
What funding for and/or people have you identified to undertake the consultation and to follow it up?

Context
Who has an interest in the consultation?
How are you going to keep them informed?
How are you going to involve them?
What else is happening in the Council in relation to your target audience and how will your work fit in?

Member involvement
How are you going to notify committees of your consultation
What member involvement would be expected or be useful?
How are you engaging member's interest and commitment?

Timescales
What time have you set aside for planning the consultation?
What timescale will suit your target audiences?
How will this timescale fit in to service and budget planning?

Knowing your target group and using a method which suits everyone's needs

Target group
Who will be affected by the outcome of the consultations now and in the long term?
Who is/are your target group(s)?

Suiting the public
What method or mix of methods are you going to use?
Will they suit people's needs?
How are you allowing for equal opportunities?

Suiting your needs
Will you be sure to get information you can use?
Will you be able to justify the information?
Are you going to do it yourself or buy in skills?

Knowing what you are going to do with what you find out

Contradictions
Are you likely to receive contradictory views and opinions? How will you deal with them?

Consider
How do you intend to use the information you receive?
Will it be the basis of service planning, specific areas of planning or simply background information?

Follow up
How have you planned to follow up the consultation issues you were looking at?
How are you going to follow up the unexpected issues people bring up?

Undertaking the consultation

Timescale
What is the timescale for carrying out the consultation?
Will this meet the needs of your target audiences?
Will it meet your service and budget planning needs?

Language
Have you allowed for the language needs of people – limited literacy, first language not English, British Sign Language, visual impairment?

Method
> What is working well and what needs to be adjusted to meet people's needs?
> What adjustments will you make?

Following up the consultattion with action

Follow up
> Are the findings clear enough or do you need to follow up with further consultation?

Service planning
> Have you used the findings to inform your service planning, including budget planning?

Ad hoc issues
> Have you followed up the issues people have raised outside the main focus of the consultation?

Let people know what is happening

Feeding back
> Have you let people know what you found out from the consultation and what you are doing with the findings?
> How will you inform people who are affected by the outcome, even if they did not take part in the consultation?

Making changes
> Have you let people know that the changes you are making result from a consultation?
> How will you make sure you continue to do this as work develops?

GIVING AND SHARING INFORMATION WITH CITIZENS

Public participation in monitoring and evaluating service quality and performance can only be successful if citizens have access to information about what our performance has been and our intended targets. Involving citizens in this aspect of a local authority's approach to reinvigorating local government is going to be a challenge now and for the foreseeable future.

Without a basic knowledge of what a local authority does it is difficult to create accountable or indeed accessible local authorities. The essence of giving and sharing information is reaching out to our citizens through publicity, exhibitions, newsletters, leaflets and increasingly through the use of information and communication technology to ensure that the public knows what we are doing.

 Task 5.1

What information does your Council provide to citizens about the quality and performance of services and how does it provide it?

Since 1993, the experience in the UK of sharing information on performance with citizens through the Audit Commission's Performance Indicators has been a complete disaster. At worst they are manipulated by the media and at best they provide isolated incidents of good performance. The move towards local performance indicators will be more helpful – but only if the performance indicators have some form of shared meaning for local people. More challenging for service managers will be the need to establish performance indicators which cut across services and perhaps different agencies.

For shared information to be meaningful to citizens and service users, it needs to be pitched at the right level using the right language and the right method. Information can be shared at the level of a community centre, neighbourhood, ethnic community, and of course across an entire locality. The information can be about specific areas of service and performance or about very broad strategic areas of service and targets. Managerial and political devolution can help managers get closer to the users of our services.

In 1994 the Royal Borough of Kingston upon Thames decided to devolve a range of decision making powers to a structure of neighbourhood committees. These comprise of all the councillors who represent the area concerned. Subject to statute and borough-wide minimum standards, neighbourhood committees are free to experiment with new initiatives and programmes. The Council believes that the neighbourhood committees result in more informed debate about Council services, performance and policies.

Tower Hamlets neighbourhood committees under the Liberal Democrats took the devolution of power to its greatest extent, with virtually all the powers of the Council that it was possible to devolve being devolved to neighbourhood committees composed of councillors for the area.

Birmingham has area committees which meet on a constituency or ward basis to consider Council issues affecting the area. More recently they have established a local action campaign, under which the Council has allocated £50 000 for each of the 39 wards, with residents having an opportunity to put forward suggestions on how the money can be spent.

South Somerset and Bradford have similar committees with budgets for specific areas of service. In this way citizens are given a real chance to make decisions by way of identifying what is needed at a local level and are given powers to allocate a minimum set of resources which can directly or indirectly impact performance in other areas. This kind of managerial and political devolution must be a key aspect of how new local government can get closer to its citizens and involve all the users of our services in taking ownership of setting priorities and targets and evaluating performance.

COMMITMENTS AND GUARANTEES

Following on from the emergence of Citizens Charters, a growing number of local authorities are, with the help and involvement of citizens and service users, establishing standards and targets for improving the performance of service delivery. Operational targets are being set at a local level to inform longer term strategic targets.

CASE STUDY: COMMITMENTS, GUARANTEES AND NEW TARGETS

LONDON BOROUGH OF TOWER HAMLETS

- An average of 189 people per day used our day centres for elders in 1997. By June 1998 this figure will have risen to 209 – a 10 per cent increase.
- In order to provide education and training for our young people during the summer, we introduced a summer university in 1995. We will attract over 2000 students.
- By March 1998 we will have attracted £23 million of external funding to transform Mile End Park into a showpiece millennium facility.
- In order to help elderly people feel more secure in their homes, we will establish a programme of security improvements for 2500 homes by April 1998.
- Ninety per cent of letters written to the Council will be responded to within 10 days of receipt of the letter – this will be achieved by March 1998.

These types of performance statements are a good example of a Council's aspirations for improving performance.

CASE STUDY: STRATEGIC COMMITMENTS

COVENTRY CITY COUNCIL

A community-wide consultation process involving a media campaign and over 100 stakeholder groups including business, community sector, religious and educational organizations, identified the following strategic priorities for the city of Coventry for a five-year period:

- Priority: create more jobs for Coventry people

- Targets: by 2003 the creation of 5000 new jobs.
- Priority: tackle crime, make communities safer
- Targets: by 2003 cut crime by 15 per cent; maintain primary detection rates for violent crimes, a minimum of 70 per cent.
- Priority: tackle poverty
- Targets: 90 per cent of people to be functionally literate and numerate by 2000; 75 per cent of 11-year-olds to reach level 4 in mathematics by 2002; reduce differences in average age of death between electoral wards by 2003 – for men, the difference should be no more than eight years, for women, the difference should be no more than seven years.
- Priority: invest in young people
- Targets: guarantee employment or training for school-leavers aged 16+ for 12 months by 2003; create and link employment and housing opportunities for 360 homeless, disadvantaged young people by 2003.
- Priority: create an exciting, vibrant city centre
- Targets: regular bus services until 2 am by 2000; 1000 new dwellings by 2003; £100 million new investment by 2003.
- Priority: meet the needs and aspirations of older people
- Targets: set up an effective forum to give older people a real voice in the city by 1999; develop a coherent strategy for older people by 2000, based on what they need and want.

MANCHESTER YOUNG PEOPLE'S COUNCIL

Manchester City Council has developed a particularly innovative way of involving young people in the work of the local authority. They have created Manchester's Young People's Council (MYPC) which is a forum for elected representatives from Manchester secondary schools, barrier-free schools and special schools. It includes co-opted members from youth projects and voluntary organizations and links directly with the Council's formal decision making process. Although in its early days, it is a mechanism for helping young people to become aware of the democratic system. The work of the MYPC and most importantly their involvement in discussions about services, policies and priorities, will enable more accurate planning of service provision for them as a target group. In turn, it will allow the Council to come back to them to review how well they have performed.

IMPLICATIONS FOR LEADING-EDGE MANAGERS

The purpose of this book is not only to introduce managers to a new performance management framework, but it is also about understanding the inter-relationships between citizen and consumer, and issues of local democracy and next generation management. It is therefore important to understand public consultation and involvement, not purely as an end in itself, but also as a major part of the performance management system. A genuinely public service needs a performance management system that will involve the public that the system seeks to serve. The next case study is a good example of a local authority's approach to community leadership and inter-agency working, leading to the identification of skills, abilities and competencies needed for the high performance of their managers. It demonstrates that when a local authority decides to turn outwards and relate more strongly to the public, it must not only re-create its organization but must develop the capacity and the skills of its members.

CASE STUDY: COVENTRY CITY COUNCIL

Coventry has a city-wide system of working and an area-based initiative focusing on areas of high disadvantage. Six areas of the city are covered, which includes over half of the population. A very successful scheme, it is an important mechanism for listening to the needs of the communities and monitoring and sharing progress. The initiative continues to be evolved across the remainder of the city, recognizing that the approach in less disadvantaged areas will require slightly different methods of working and involvement.

Each area generally covers two electoral wards and has an area co-ordinator employed by the city Council. Its role is to develop community-led, needs-based planning for local communities. A principal task of the area coordinator is to promote and lead inter-agency ways of working with communities including the police, health service and voluntary organizations. An area team includes a social services officer and housing officer. From time to time other officers with particular disciplines are brought in to help; for example an environment person for a 'greening' scheme. Teams consist of between 10 and 15 individuals. The core of the team – the area coordinator, the administrator and community safety officer – are employed on permanent contracts. The rest of the team are brought together from across other agencies and stakeholders within the area, creating a virtual team.

The team has some very small local budgets; most work will be undertaken by influencing and negotiating with other service departments and agencies to release finances and resources to support developments in local action plans. Team members from other agencies work with their own organizations to influence the release of resources for community development.

The area teams are supported by activity groups for particular issues, for example support for children under 8 years of age and community safety.

This way of working presents a major cultural shift for Coventry, requiring officers to focus on service delivery on a needs and area basis. Team members take collective responsibility for actions and share decision making across agencies – a very different way of working from the traditional departmental structures of local authorities. Team members work as part of a virtual cross-service team, which is considerably more challenging than being part of a loose grouping or working party.

The list below, taken from Hayden (1997), illustrates the competencies required for area coordinators. These associated skills and abilities are relevant for leading-edge managers, whatever your service area.

Planning	Establishes processes for developing area plans, and plans activities to achieve the area objectives
Evaluation	Continuously reviews and seeks to improve the quality of service based on regular monitoring of progress towards the achievement of planned outcomes
Coordination	Makes sure agencies which serve the area work together in the best interests of the local community
Empowerment	Encourages and enables others to take control of and responsibility for their actions
Local needs analysis	Gathering and interpreting information about the needs of the area so as to identify the priorities and focus for the work of local agencies
Problem solving	Develops practical solutions in response to identified problems or issues
Influencing/negotiating	Gains the agreement and commitment of people to ideas and to work towards achieving the objectives of the area plan
Team development	Creates and sustains an environment conducive to joint working, recognizing and harnessing the capabilities of others while developing peoples skills and knowledge

| Political nous | Uses and understands the formal and informal power relationships within the area so as to get things done |
| Drive | Achieves results through personal commitment, energy and enthusiasm, demonstrating a will to succeed. |

HOW THE PUBLIC PRIORITIZES LOCAL AUTHORITY SERVICES

In 1997 the LGA commissioned a MORI poll asking people to rate which of a range of local services were the most important to them. The findings provide important information for all local authority managers about what the public's priorities are.

Service	per cent
Crime/law and order	75
Fire service	64
Refuse collection	61
Parks, open space and trees	50
Street lighting	49
Street cleaning	49
Road maintenance	49
Primary schools	45
Secondary schools	45
Pavement maintenance	44

Thinking about local services, which of these are most important to you?

Priority	per cent
Working to reduce crime	29
Attracting new jobs and businesses to the area	27
Improving education standards	21
Keeping Council Tax levels down	21
Ensuring that everyone has decent housing	19
Providing care services for the elderly, disabled and children	18
Protecting and improving the environment	13
Improving the public transport system	8
Don't know	1

From this list, what would you like to be the top priority for your local Council?

Three-quarters of people (75 per cent) rated services to tackle crime and law and order as important to them and, in a different question, working to reduce crime came out as people's top priority for their local Council. High ratings for fire services (64 per cent) and street lighting (49 per cent) when thinking about what services are most important to them, further emphasize how much people value services that make them feel safer in their neighbourhood.

Apart from these issues, it is largely the most visible services that people are likely to regard as important. Six out of ten people place a high value on refuse collection (61 per cent), with half making a priority of parks, open spaces and trees (50 per cent), 49 per cent choosing street cleaning and 49 per cent choosing road maintenance. Nearly half of respondents (45 per cent) named primary and secondary schools as their priority.

When asked to identify the single issue that they would like to see as a top priority for their local Council, attracting new jobs and businesses to the area (27 per cent) was a close second to wanting to reduce crime (29 per cent). They also rated improving education standards (21 per cent), ensuring that everyone has decent housing (19 per cent) and providing care services for the elderly, disabled and children (18 per cent) as the most important priorities. Keeping Council Tax levels down was the priority for 21 per cent of people, indicating the importance of balancing high quality service provision with value for money.

These important national issues – safety, health, education, jobs, housing and the environment – are at the heart of local government in Britain today. While these priorities may change over time, it is essential for a manager who is genuinely concerned about performance to ensure that he or she understands the priorities of citizens.

BEST VALUE AND CONSULTATION

Best value is a major new policy introduced in British local government in 1998. It provides a national framework for local authorities to achieve quality. However, in line with the argument in this chapter, it recognizes that a public sector manager can only manage performance or in this case manage the provision of value if he or she fully involves citizens. It is therefore more than just about economy and efficiency and is about how democratically we involve citizens who are also our customers in setting priorities, shaping services and measuring our performance. The best value framework emphasizes local choice, local accountability and a creative environment, seeking to achieve constant improvements.

The best value framework places a duty on each local authority to publicly demonstrate best value in the provision of its services. The framework promotes local choice and diversity and accountability through local authority

Table 5.2   *Managers best value checklist (adapted from Birmingham City Council)*

Best Value Agenda	Implications and Actions
Challenge	
☐ Why do we do what we do?	☐
☐ How do we measure the value of what we do?	☐
☐ What do citizens, service users/ partners really want?	☐
☐ How can we involve councillors in challenging performance?	☐
Compare	
☐ What should we be comparing?	☐
☐ Who should we compare ourselves with and how?	☐
☐ What indicators should we use (inside and outside)?	☐
☐ How do we get behind the figures and discover the best practice?	☐
Consult	
☐ Who should we be consulting with?	☐
☐ How do we get communities involved in measurement of performance?	☐
☐ What ways should we use to consult with customers?	☐
Compete	
☐ Are we competitive enough?	☐
☐ Are our working patterns flexible enough?	☐
☐ Can we be expected to consider the externalization of our services?	☐
Climate	
☐ Are we able to get the best out of our people?	☐

Table 5.2 *(contd)*

☐ Do we value managers as coaches and change leaders?	☐
☐ Are we serious about achieving real measurable improvements?	☐
☐ How do we get wider ownership for best value principles and putting forward values in action?	☐
Culture	
☐ What barriers do we need to overcome in seeking to achieve a flexible and responsive organization?	☐
☐ How do we ensure the commitment needed for continous service improvement and change?	☐
☐ How do we deal with reluctance to accept any necessary break with the past?	☐
☐ How do we encourage support for a shared vision of the future?	☐
Competence	
☐ Do we have the skills as members to work in a best value way?	☐
☐ Are we serious about creating responsible managers?	☐
☐ Do we have the skills to measure achievement and share good practice?	☐
☐ Have we got the right people doing the right things?	☐

service plans developed in consultation with and supported by other service users and providers.

Best value aims to improve services by:

● challenging their relevance;
● comparing them with the best;

- consulting with the public;
- encouraging the delivery of services which compete with the best.

The next generation management tools, techniques and approaches that this book explores are largely about meeting this agenda. Leading-edge managers will know and understand that best value as a way of working will embrace and touch upon all Council activities. They understand that the framework

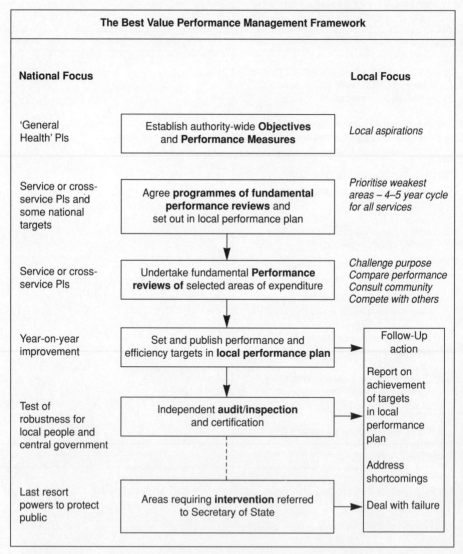

Figure 5.1 *Best value performance management framework (Department of Environment, Transport and the Regions, 1998)*

that has been established will also help them to reflect back to local people the relevance of local government. Best value provides a vehicle for community participation and empowerment.

In terms of the new performance management framework, there is an exact fit between the requirements of the best value regime and the various arenas that Councils need to address to improve their performance.

The best value performance management framework

The performance management framework for best value put forward by the government is a very high level framework; it is shown in Figure 5.1.

In gearing up to meet the requirements of this performance management framework, local authorities will have to devise a coherent and holistic approach to performance management. The new performance management framework suggested in Chapter 3 outlines the different arenas of activity that a local authority must be involved in to have a balanced approach and to meet the requirements set out above. Here we have learnt that it is impossible to manage the performance of public services without some understanding of the involvement of citizens.

 Task 5.2

Discuss the questions listed in the best value managers' checklist with colleagues in your team. What are the implications and actions for you?

SUMMARY

In this chapter we have explored how citizens can make a significant contribution to performance management in local government at an operational and strategic level. We have recognized that consultation and involvement with citizens is a key element of a coherent and holistic approach to performance management. Best practice for consulting citizens, and the implications for and skills needed by leading-edge managers have been outlined. Just as importantly the link between the best value regime and the importance of managers engaging with citizens has been made.

In Chapter 6 we explore performance management from a strategic and corporate point of view and make the links between strategic management of the Council and service delivery.

REFERENCES

DETR (1998) *Modernizing Local Government: Improving local services through best value*, TSO, Norwich.

Hayden, C (1997) Area co-ordinator's competency file.

Rawson, M (1997) *A Consultation Strategy*, Coventry City Council.

6 Macro performance

This chapter deals with the critical mechanisms and tools that must be in place and available to ensure that the local authority can be managed strategically at a member and officer level. It is an overview of what we mean by strategy in local government, the ways of working, some of the key tools and techniques for next generation management. These are essential to create a firm 'managerial grip' on the organization, which cannot be achieved unless all of the different levels of performance management interlock.

It is usual for such chapters to be written for managers who work in the strategic or corporate centre of the local authority. This chapter about strategic management has, however, been written for leading-edge managers across the local authority who are responsible for developing, delivering and facilitating services. For while it is not the responsibility of middle managers to construct the entire strategy for a local authority, it is important that they both understand the whole process and play their appropriate part in its creation. This chapter is for managers who will be involved in facilitating the development of choices, and ways in which services should be planned and delivered.

Macro performance concerns the capability of a total organization. This totality includes not only those inside the organization but also those we work with across sectors and on an inter-agency basis. All of these partners, together, provide the capability to deliver strategic priorities at all levels, from Council-wide right down to area and neighbourhood levels.

Macro performance is not necessarily about strategic management alone. Macro performance should be a term associated with next generation management because it focuses on the big picture, beyond the Council. Society has undergone two decades of incredible change which has not only affected local government, but has changed the societal context generally.

In an age when local authorities at unitary level are responsible for constructing over 50 statutory plans and dozens of locally initiated plans and strategies, next generation management must find ways of synchronizing these plans without overtly trying to manage and coordinate perfect relationships. The emphasis must be on coordination or alignment of all of these plans, not control.

In Chapter 4 the illustration of a nest of plans was used, reflecting the need to make links between vision, corporate, area, departmental and service plans, right down to team and individual priorities. The LGMB's survey on organizational change (1996) asked a number of questions about the evaluation of performance within their authorities. Two-thirds of the respondents judged that the present level was inadequate in terms of establishing efficiency levels, whether objectives have been met, which groups have benefited most from services, the quality of service, whether standards are adequate, and whether Council policies have been achieved in practice.

Table 6.1 shows that around half of all authorities attribute a major role to these considerations, with the notable exception of establishing which groups have benefited from services, where 62 per cent reported a minor role, and 24 per cent no role at all. Table 6.2 shows how the importance of evaluation work has increased in recent years, especially for service managers, chief officers and members.

Table 6.1   *The role of performance evaluation in the authority (Sanderson et al, 1998)*

	Major Role %	Minor Role %	None %
Establishing efficiency levels	43	42	4
Establishing whether objectives have been met	63	33	4
Establishing which groups have benefited most	14	62	24
Establishing quality of service	54	43	4
Establishing whether service standards are adequate	46	50	5
Establishing whether policies have been achieved	55	40	5

As we move into an era requiring us to be more focused on best value, the LGMB study reflects a challenging situation for leading-edge managers. They will have to inspire citizens to become involved in local government, and elected members in paying more attention to the way we evaluate what we have or have not achieved.

Table 6.2 *The importance of evaluation change over the last three years*
(Sanderson et al, *1998)*

	Increase %	Remained about the same %	Decrease %
Importance to members	60	39	1
Importance to chief officers	72	27	1
Importance to service managers	72	27	1

STRATEGY AND MACRO PERFORMANCE

In earlier chapters we have talked about the need to develop a performance management strategy and action plans to move forward and meet the challenges of new local government. Performance in new local government can only be successful if it recognizes that it must encompass some very wide issues of strategy. Next generation management will look to strategy for the long term prosperity and survival of both the Council and the communities it serves. In the context of performance management a strategy will enable us to look forward to where we want to be in three, five, ten years time.

The failing of the old local government approach to strategy is that it has been a short term one. Often I have been involved in meetings with members and officers who talk about a strategy for the next 12 months. Focusing on short term issues in a strategy will inevitably lead the local authority to make short term opportunistic decisions that will exclude any real strategic consideration in the longer term. Given the importance of long term change to Councils and their communities, such an approach will lack any coherence or consistency in terms of where the local authority wants to be. Therefore in the context of performance management our strategy is concerned with where we want to be in five or ten years' time. Clearly such long term strategic planning is important for major resource allocation and resource-switching decisions.

An aspect of strategy that most managers don't consider is the need to achieve concentration of effort. Concentration on priority issues, ways of working, economies of scale, values and goals is all-important when we begin to develop a strategy to move forward. In this way a strategy can be more effective and our performance higher. A good example of concentration would be how well a local authority could focus the attention of all its resources, its staff and its ways of working on a number of fixed strategic priorities and targets over a defined period.

MACRO PERFORMANCE AND STRATEGIC CONTROL

For Council members on service committees, working groups and officers within service arenas, 'strategic control' is the last thing they want to hear about. However, it is an important element of macro performance. If, in terms of the direction of the authority, there were no strategic control, what would be the purpose of a corporate or strategic centre? Strategic control doesn't mean a huge central department telling others what to do. Strategic control is about taking up and advocating those priorities and targets, agreed through consultation and involvement, inside and outside the Council, across services and across the agencies at neighbourhood and city-wide level. Strategic control must take these priorities and ensure that the organization understands that these are the key performance requirements. They need to be continually reconfirmed, so that they will remain as a significant part of the Council's agenda. There will be many more priorities and targets across different committees and different service areas. So, local authorities will need to focus and concentrate their efforts and energies to achieve longer term goals that in return should be connected to all levels of the Council's work.

I recently heard of a private sector organization which had more than 1000 key performance measures. The organization was spread across three continents. Business units were totally autonomous, yet they all had the same branding. What the board began to recognize was that although this had been a successful way of working for many years, there was a lack of coherence within the organization and performance was declining. Investigation showed that the lack of corporate targets for all of their devolved business units, together with the lack of corporate organizational values, was leading to different parts of the business across the world moving in separate directions. To remedy this, 14 corporate performance measures and a set of values were agreed. In this way the strategic centre of this particular organization advocated a form of strategic control which resulted in greater coherence and increased returns.

Key aspects of macro performance

Macro performance must include a review of the processes that are used for policy and service development and implementation. These processes must be able to ensure that there is a strong relationship between the high-level performance needs of the organization and plans for specific services. The systems must ensure that these different levels work together.

Below is an outline of key elements managers need to consider when putting together a service plan. The guidance has been adapted from Warwickshire County Council's Service Planning Guide for Managers (1992).

Table 6.3 *Tips for making strategic control work*

Selecting the right objectives
- These should be based on political priorities and citizens' views.
- Don't go mad: select a limited number of priorities with a range of targets.
- Identify key milestones, enabling you to measure short-term progress.

Setting suitable targets
- These should be specific and objectively measurable.
- Where possible, managers directly responsible for delivering the targets should be involved in constructing them; at the same time they must stretch the managers.
- Comparative information should be available to enable you to measure performance against the targets agreed.

Ensuring performance
- Organize a planned monitoring and evaluation process as part of the service planning and performance management systems of the Council.
- Do not be fearful of strategic intervention where performance is poor and failing.

Macro performance capability
- You must have high quality people facilitating the development of your performance management policy and resources processes.
- Your capability should be people who are facilitators and see service areas as their customers.
- Planning processes must be transparent; members must understand them.

Keeping things simple
- Do not accept extremely lengthy technical reports when evaluating strategic priorities and targets.
- Ensure that people involved in making things happen and delivering the targets are involved in giving face-to-face feedback as part of the performance management process.
- Use formal as well as informal processes for performance management reviews.

Key elements of a service plan

- *Executive summary.* This gives the key points of the plan at a glance: nature of the business; mission statement; indication of main pressures for change; strategy for responding to these pressures; and main objectives for the year.
- *External analysis (opportunities and threats).* The context in which the service operates. The important things to note are the trends taking place outside the unit which may affect it. What are the short, medium and long term pressures?
- *Customers.* 'Customers' here includes anyone who receives a service from the unit, or is affected by its actions. It may include members, staff in other departments. Remember, citizens are customers and vice versa.
- *Demand for service.* This builds on the analysis of customers, with an indication of the type and level of demand on the service unit from each client group. Where appropriate, there should be an indication of the different types of service demanded by one particular client group, as well as an

indication of groups who are not using the service, because they are unaware that it is available, or because it is difficult or inaccessible to them.

- *Other sources of supply.* Where appropriate, an indication of other sources of supply of the kind of service the unit has to offer. Is there any competition? If so, what is it?
- *Corporate strategy.* An indication of how the service units' priorities will contribute to the Council's strategic/corporate priorities and targets.
- *Political environment.* What is happening at central and local government level which may affect the work of the service unit?
- *Restraints.* Those factors which restrict the freedom to take certain actions.
- *Communications internal/external.* How the unit communicates with its customers, both directly and indirectly. How the work of the unit is perceived by various groups. Where there is a need to address misunderstandings, to boost or to lessen demand, or to raise the profile of the unit, and how this will be achieved.
- *Alternative delivery mechanisms.* How the business service could be delivered differently to meet the best value and social justice targets of the Council, either by the Council itself or through a joint venture or trust, partnership, etc.
- *Internal analysis (strengths and weaknesses).* In order to respond positively to external forces, various changes may need to be made in the way the unit works, to increase efficiency, etc.
- *Performance and productivity – comparative information.* How well has the unit performed over the last year? How well equipped is it to respond to the challenges it is likely to have to meet over the period of the plan? How does its efficiency or output compare with similar units in other departments or authorities? How cost-effective is the unit?
- *Performance management.* An indication of the level of quality of service provided and how this matches with service user expectations. Is the level of quality in each area consistent? Management arrangements should exist to ensure consistency.
- *Staffing.* What are the unit's strengths and weaknesses with regard to staff? Are there any particular skills that need to be developed or capitalized on? What are the unit's training and development needs? What recruitment or retention needs are there?
- *Accommodation.* Are there any factors relating to accommodation which may affect the unit's ability to perform over the period of the plan?
- *Technology.* The level and use of technology within the unit and whether it needs to be developed or updated. Training and equipment needs in the short, medium and long term.
- *Relationship with external suppliers.* Where relevant, the unit's policy towards external suppliers.

The plan

Your business or service delivery plan will need some kind of structure. The following is a suggested format.

- *Introduction.* Purpose of plan, background to its production, structure of the plan.
- *Statement of beliefs and values.* Where appropriate, a sentence or two spelling out the principles under which the unit operates. For example: 'To behave towards all people with respect and regard to their social status, gender, ethnic origin or ability' (Probation Service).
- *Strategic direction.* A summary of management principles underlying the objectives set for the year. This section would indicate the general thrust of the response to pressures for change – the strategic direction of the unit.
- *Objectives.* What needs to be done over the period covered by the plan for the strategic direction of the unit. Where relevant, an indication of the priorities of those objectives.
- *Key tasks.* A more specific indication of what needs to be done to achieve the objectives. Where relevant, an indication of the various rankings of key tasks.
- *Performance indicators.* Performance indicators should be defined for each proposed activity of the unit, including those normally seen as routine. How the indicators will be monitored so that they can be used as part of a future planning process.
- *Resource implications.* The amount of staff time and any other resource that will be devoted to meeting each objective.
- *Budget.* Setting out in more detail the distribution of financial resources throughout the unit. For a business unit, forecasting the likely level of income from a particular level of demand.
- *Capital requirements.* Where appropriate, the present and future capital requirements of the unit.
- *Human resources.* Numbers of staff and levels of skills (recruitment and retention needs).
- *Information systems.* Any information systems that need to be put in place or modified to monitor the plan and communicate its implementation.

The service plan is a critical document to be produced by managers; it will be used for reviewing the performance of your service or area of work and setting its future direction.

The following case study presents us with an interesting comparison of different issues that need to be considered at a macro level (strategic and corporate) and operational level when formulating service delivery plans.

CASE STUDY: CREATING PERFORMANCE PLANS BUILDING ON EXISTING PLANS AND PROCESSES

TORFAEN COUNTY BOROUGH COUNCIL

Torfaen have a community plan and a service delivery plan. To meet the best value principles their overall objective is to involve communities and key stakeholders in determining objectives for the authority.

Service delivery plans – these are individual service strategies developed by chief officers. They are forwarded to 10 identified key stakeholders for each of the major service areas for their observations and discussion. These are incorporated into a full draft of a service delivery plan.

Community plans – directors draw up preliminary discussion papers, drawing out key issues for their services within different communities. Community focus groups are brought together for each of the major geographical areas. The issues are discussed in terms of local and overall priorities and how these might be met. Priorities and targets are evolved.

The next stage of the process is to pull together the two documents into a single draft plan that is then circulated to a wide range of individuals and community organizations, stakeholders, etc. Comments are incorporated into the draft plans and those consulted have the opportunity of meeting with the Council to further influence and negotiate priorities and targets.

Issues that Torfaen have had to consider include:

- Options for meaningful evaluation and review within the consultation process.
- The governance of Torfaen.
- How other agencies are involved in dovetailing their plans and policies.
- The incorporation of statutory plans into the planning process, for example housing strategy, social care plan, the economic development plan.
- Synchronizing timing with other agencies in terms of their planning processes.
- Financial planning, linking the planning process with the budget setting process.
- Service and organizational development plans – these are detailed internal plans that need to link upwards and downwards with the community and service delivery plan.
- Performance review and quality planning – to integrate the agreed performance management strategy with the policy and financial planning processes.

- Service reviews – the prioritization of service reviews within the planning process and the need to link with the best value framework.
- Management and staff development – the training strategy to develop the capability of managers to meet the authority's business objectives.

This long list of issues considered by Torfaen in evolving their current planning systems to take on board a performance plan arising from the best value regime is a reflection of the complexities and inter-relationships involved. Next generation management will need to find ways of cutting through these issues if managers are not to be dogged by bureaucracy and meaningless paper-chasing exercises.

The best value regime will bring many challenges for local government in terms of their macro planning. All Councils must review their planning processes, underpinning their capacity to meet best value requirements:

- Putting citizens first and being accountable for the services provided.
- Working in partnership with other key stakeholders.
- Setting objectives, identifying priority services and activities, and allocating resources to them, taking into account the medium and longer term financial implications for both revenue and capital.
- Having in place mechanisms for monitoring and reviewing performance and setting improvement targets.

ASSESSING PERFORMANCE AT DIFFERENT LEVELS

It is vital that strategic management can assess performance at every level of the organization. The matrix in Table 6.4, taken from *Made to Measure – Evaluation in practice in local government* (Sanderson *et al*, 1998), reflects very usefully the different levels of performance, macro to micro, within an organization. It is also emphasizes the link between monitoring and review which is not easily demonstrated in the new performance management framework described in Chapter 3.

RESOURCE SWITCHING

All of these planning mechanisms are only really important if they lead to different activity. All too often the planning mechanism itself is seen as the end result of the entire process. A manager can feel that a good plan is good enough. Obviously this is insufficient. Unless planning leads to different activity, it has simply been a justification of the status quo. So, for the rest of

Table 6.4 *Assessing performance at different 'levels' (Sanderson* et al, *1998)*

	Aproach to assessing performance	
	Monitoring ──────────►	Review
Locality	**Partnership strategy** ● Key objectives/issues/PIs	**Evaluation** ● Impact/contribution of joint working
Authority	**Strategic/Corporate plan** ● Key service objectives/issues/PIs	
Functional division	**Committee plan** ● Key service objectives/issues/PIs	**Performance review** ● Achievement/impact/added value
Service	**Committee/Service/Business plan** ● Service objectives/issues/PIs	**Service review** ● Achievement/impact/added value
Provider unit	**Business plan/contract** ● Service specification	● Process/implementation
Individual	**Action plan/task specification** ● Defined tasks/milestones	**Staff appraisal process**

this chapter I will outline the different way in which macro planning can lead to very different outcomes, starting with the switching of resources.

Macro performance will involve organizations, at a corporate level, switching resources from one area of activity to another to meet the changing needs and priorities of the organization and the changing needs and demands of local communities. It is a fact that no matter how fixed budgets seem to be within service areas, departments and teams, managers are innovative enough to find ways of re-directing resources. New local government will require more openness and transparency in terms of how we spend public money and the reasons for switching from one area of activity to another. Clearly, through the processes of citizen involvement in setting priorities and targets, we can justify much of what is done.

Local government is big business. Our resources can be used to pump-prime a wide range of activities to make even greater things happen for our communities. Although we should not be constrained by bureaucratic and inflexible ways of resource-switching, I believe that at a macro level, next generation management will require us to have agreed ways of resource-switching that can be explained in a coherent way to our citizens. Too often, at a corporate level, directors with responsibility for these processes design and re-design sometimes rather sophisticated and sometimes over-simplified processes that are driven not by resource-switching but the reduction of budgets. They range at worst from pro rata cuts resulting in the worst areas of deprivation suffering even more, and at best in helping stagger the approach to planned cuts.

The 'decision conferencing' technique helps decision makers explore and come to understand their beliefs, professional judgements and preferences in the context of the particular choices facing them. The decision makers are helped by a facilitator and an analyst through structural workshops. This has been a particularly useful approach for a number of local authorities; Dudley Metropolitan District Council has made good use of it.

Weaver and Morgan (1993) describe a decision workshop as a structured meeting, based on the decision conferencing process. There are meetings, generally lasting two days, at which all the 'owners' of a problem gather together to agree upon a solution.

In the workshop, the participants first identify their key service areas and the resources currently committed to each, and then the service implications of varying that resource by a significant amount (say 5, 10, 20 per cent or more). So that a budget can be constructed that best meets the aims of the Council, the participants then agree criteria that encapsulate the benefits that the resource usage should achieve. These will be used to evaluate the pros and cons of putting more (or less) resource in to a particular service.

ALTERNATIVE DELIVERY MECHANISMS

In investigating the whole area of macro performance it becomes apparent that improvement in service quality and performance should not have boundaries. It is inevitable that if a local authority genuinely reviews all of its services with a strategic aim of improving them, they will create new forms of service delivery. For example, we should not only consider ways of making things happen inside the Council but next generation management will be concerned with going through organizational service and cross-sectoral barriers to ensure new ways of working are explored and tested for their appropriateness to citizens' needs. This must involve working outside the Council as well as inside. Alongside this will be judgements concerned with efficiency, effectiveness, equality and social value. There are many different ways of delivering services and making things happen for our citizens.

The concept of best value has resulted in a significant challenge to local authorities. This challenge concerns the service delivery options for which local authorities have opted. Best value means asking local authorities to examine whether alternative ways of delivering services are available. Local authorities must demonstrate to their own auditors' satisfaction that a range of service delivery models have been considered and that the chosen option represents best value against pre-determined evaluation criteria.

The options to be considered will range from in-house provision through partnerships with voluntary, public and private sector organizations, to outsourcing. The final option would be a decision to not provide a service that is discretionary and is perceived not to be providing best value.

New local government will need to be innovative in developing their responses to best value. Clearly benchmarking (which is discussed in Chapter 7) will be a key tool in comparing costs of service provision or staffing and output levels. Benchmarking will also become useful in terms of evaluating similar service delivery models between authorities on a like-for-like basis.

The private sector is now fully aware of the opportunities that the introduction of best value offers. They are looking for and bringing forward a new range of service delivery mechanisms that will yield profits. Local authorities are obliged to consider these alongside the more traditional service delivery models. A range of different models includes:

- private finance initiatives
- joint ventures
- external contractors
- industrial and providence societies
- local authority companies
- voluntary tendering
- housing associations
- housing companies
- large scale voluntary transfer
- consortia
- charitable trusts.

Clearly in looking at different service delivery options, members and officers will need to consider the implications for both present and future service provision for their citizens. All options carry a degree of risk, which will vary depending on the potential service provider, the nature of the service itself, and its relative importance. What appears to represent best value one day may not on a future occasion.

 Task 6.1

What alternative service delivery mechanisms does your local authority use? How do these approaches add value for citizens?

STRATEGIC ALLIANCES AND PARTNERSHIPS

New local government will search more rigorously for alternative delivery mechanisms that reflect better value for our citizens. However, as well as the perceived benefits of value for money, increased productivity, lower over-heads and so on, there can be many pitfalls in pursuing 'harder' partnerships such as joint ventures. The following principles, although designed for use when considering joint ventures, are applicable in many cases to other types of harder partnerships.

Key principle: Partnerships will be progressed if they represent the most suitable means of pursuing the Council's objectives
A feasibility review is prepared before a joint venture solution is progressed. This results in a committee report identifying:

- the objectives of the joint venture;
- alternative options, and why a partnership is the preferred approach;
- a financial appraisal;
- other implications and an assessment of risk.

Key principle: The Council selects the right partners
- Partners are sought who empathize with and perhaps share the Council's aims and objectives.
- Partners must have adequate experience, technical capability and financial strength to meet the partnership objectives.

Key principle: Competition is the best way to achieve value for money
- open competition is used to select partners wherever practical;
- as much information as possible is shared with potential partners in a competition;
- information is sought and supplied by formal, methodical processes;
- competitive interest is maintained until maximum agreement is achieved on commercial principles;
- external financial advisers are employed where competition cannot be achieved.

Key principle: Joint ventures are progressed in a well-managed way
- the Council determines its requirements before seeking a partner;
- all joint ventures are progressed by a project team, under a project officer, plus (at a minimum) legal and financial support;
- project teams share a commitment to the objectives of the project;
- project officers are responsible for effective project and timetable manage-ment;

- communication takes place with affected staff;
- commercial agreements are recorded in comprehensive 'heads of terms' agreements before preferred partners are formally selected.

Key principle: Members give strategic advice on joint ventures

- members receive the results of a feasibility review in committee and decide whether to proceed further;
- members receive periodic progress reports when a joint venture is being pursued;
- a comprehensive financial report is required before joint ventures are concluded;
- members continue to exercise strategic oversight of the Council's on-going involvement in joint ventures.

Key principle: The Council seeks to use its capital resources to best effect

- this usually means the city Council holds only a minority interest in joint venture companies; otherwise, a joint venture company must constrain its activities to minimize the capital 'score'.

Key principle: The Council wishes to protect its investment and other interests in joint venture companies

Key principle: The Council wishes to promote good governance of its joint venture companies

- governance of companies is as open as possible, commensurate with the need for commercial confidentiality and best private sector practice;
- companies linked with the Council set high standards of ethical behaviour and financial management;
- best private sector practice is promoted in the employment of executive directors;
- best private sector practice is promoted in reporting company performance;
- companies are subject to effective audit;
- the use of independent non-executive directors is a valuable tool.

Key principle: Risks are explicitly identified and managed

- risks, which may be financial or non-financial, are identified as early in the process as possible, and fully explained to members;
- risks are allocated between partners, ie, it is decided which partner(s) takes action or suffers loss if a future event happens;
- risks are allocated to the partner most able to influence an outcome, while ensuring a fair deal for all parties;

- business plans are prepared by the party bearing the business risk (before a preferred partner is selected). They are scrutinized by the Council;
- a process is agreed for managing those risks allocated to the Council.

Key principle: The Council learns from its experiences
- a review of the process takes place after the conclusion of each joint venture agreement.

Macro performance and strategic alliances

The phrase 'strategic alliances' describes a form of partnership with the private sector, or collaboration between types of public organizations seeking mutual benefits. Local authorities have been building partnerships for many years, however, strategic alliances are more than the soft partnerships of the last 10 to 15 years. Strategic alliances concern the longer term relationships between organizations. In many instances the values and objectives of the organizations with which local authorities seek to develop alliances will be similar to those of the local authority. For example, an alliance between the Council's IT service and the contracting division of a large private sector organization will be based on improving service quality and customer care, etc. Yet, they will also have slightly different values when it comes to issues to do with profit.

Alliances concern mergers between organizations that represent more complex links between different types of service organizations. Leading-edge managers will think more strategically in terms of the future positioning of the services they are managing, and recognize the need to build relationships and alliances inside and outside the organization for the future development of their service areas. Just as economic development areas of Councils foster relationships with local authorities in countries abroad looking for inward investment opportunities, so too will leading-edge managers in the future, positioning services more competitively to meet the needs of citizens in a best value way.

SUMMARY

In this chapter we have considered the critical mechanisms that need to be in place and available to ensure that the local authority can be managed strategically at a member and officer level. The contributions of service managers across the Council, partners, external agencies and citizens are all acknowledged as being vital to achieving strategic priorities at all levels.

Macro performance concerns the total capability of the organization and therefore is not necessarily about strategic management alone.

In Chapter 7 we will discuss the role of information and performance measurement in securing an effective performance management system.

REFERENCES

LGMB (1996) Survey of Organizational Change, LGMB, London.

Sanderson, I, Bovaird, T, Martin, S and Foreman, A (1998) *Made to Measure – Evaluation in practice in local government*, LGMB, London.

Warwickshire County Council (1992) *Guide to Service Planning for Managers*, Warwickshire County Council.

Weaver, M and Morgan, T (1993) 'Budget making – is there a better way?', *Public Finance and Accountancy*, June, pp 52–55.

7 Information and performance measurement

This chapter is essentially concerned with the importance of information and performance measurement within a Council's overall performance management framework. At a basic level, managers simply must know how their staff and services are performing against local and national comparatives. New local government will require leading-edge managers to be open and transparent about their performance, holding themselves accountable for what is or is not achieved. The best value regime demands this of all services. Accurate, relevant, timely information about performance becomes an imperative for next generation management.

The performance measurement process is not simply a technical one. Operational managers must know what to measure, how to measure and how and when to communicate messages about performance. The journey to becoming a high performing, modern local authority will require leading-edge managers to question and analyse their own values, insights, emotions and ability to gain knowledge and apply themselves to changing circumstances.

This book demonstrates that it is extremely challenging to put in place a coherent approach to performance management in new local government. Although this has always been the case, the challenge is even greater in new networked organizations. Despite the challenge, it is an essential component of a public service since the public needs to know whether you are spending their money wisely; without that knowledge they will never be able to fully trust government.

Given the importance of values for a manager, he or she not only needs to know the values of the local authority but also has to appreciate whether his or her own values fit in with them.

In next generation management, information in all its forms will be critical as it contributes to the creation of knowledge of staff, elected members and citizens. Knowledge or 'intellectual capital' is the most undisclosed and under-used element of resource management within local government. Leading-edge managers will be so passionate about the search for relevant, accurate and timely information that their peers will question the value of time and energy being invested in this activity. However, leading-edge managers will understand and recognize that without data, performance measurement is a worthless, subjective and parochial activity. New local government must operate on a network basis inside and outside our organizations.

Strategic, corporate and operational information will be required about performance measures and indicators at different levels for different purposes. The coordinated and coherent management of the work of local government will require managers who have access to information and who value knowledge as a resource.

This chapter discusses the contribution of information and communication technology to the governance of new local government. It is also discussed in terms of listening and involving citizens, particularly with regard to our performance. A significant part of the chapter is concerned with the concept of performance measures, performance indicators and perhaps more significantly methods for measuring performance, including the purpose and concept of benchmarking.

THE AGE OF COMMUNICATION AND INFORMATION TECHNOLOGY

As information and communication technology evolves, its developers are concerned with the integration and compatibility of different levels of information. This has to take place at a macro and micro level, whether the macro is at international or council-wide level, and whether the micro is at service delivery unit or neighbourhood level. This business approach to the linkages between different levels means that the development of information technology platforms within local government are more likely to be compatible with a wider band of technologies. As the production of microchips becomes ever more efficient, the basic components of IT systems will become cheaper. To move organizations forward to become knowledge-based, investment needs to be made *now* in transforming the organization to one that can use information. There is a need to be more effective in the use of information; many local government managers feel overloaded with information that they see as irrelevant.

There is a vast amount of information in local authorities, most of it inaccessible. Local authorities rarely recognize the value of such information. A unique commercial company has been launched by the Local Government Management Board called the Local Government Information House Ltd

(LGIH). They understand that the value of data held by local authorities has been recognized by the commercial sector.

In the late 1990s more than 45 companies are estimated to have asked for copies of local government data registers every day, using the citizens' access to public information rights contained in the Copyright Act. These rights do not extend to the further copying and commercial exploitation of the data – which is going on. Local authorities are foregoing potential licence income. The LGIH provides a flexible way for local government to deal in the information market without imposing legal risks or administrative burdens on individual Councils. The LGIH is an innovative approach to supporting local government in using more effectively the data it holds, and raising income in the process.

Next generation management will have to understand the information management requirements of organization in terms of its governance role and issues to do with performance. IT is a means of harnessing and using more efficiently and effectively this information, but it is not the only means.

Information is also power to each authority. All local government is good at keeping information to themselves, whether it is at a departmental or service level. It is imperative that this form of protection is broken down. These attitudes must be challenged to enable managers to work across services more effectively.

Next generation management will need to look at the information needs of local authorities from the following viewpoints:

- strategic foresight – information to make decisions for the future;
- service quality and performance – different levels of information for making judgements about the quality of service delivery and performance of individuals, teams and the organization as a whole;
- civic leadership and governance – ways of involving the public in identifying priorities, sharing information, shaping services, monitoring and reviewing service quality and performance.

 Task 7.1

How could you develop an information culture, where information is treated seriously, valued and of relevance to the purpose and core values of your Council's work?

Tips for undertaking an information audit

It is vital to start the process of using information by first finding out what information exists within the authority. Few local authorities actually know what they know about their communities and their service users. This can lead to the organization spending a great deal of time and money finding out what they already know. An information audit therefore makes good economic sense, and should cover:

- the type of information that is held;
- where information is held and whether it is on a database, in a filing system, etc;
- whether it is structured or unstructured;
- how up to date it is;
- how fragmented the information may be;
- whether it duplicates other information;
- whether it is consistent with other information;
- what privacy and security arrangements exist;
- who manages and maintains it – if indeed it is maintained;
- who needs it, how they gain access and what for;
- how much it is used.

(Source: Wedgewood Oppenheimer, 1996)

The audit can be utilized to produce directories of information holdings to be published inside and possibly outside the local authority.

The measurement of performance is an important part of the overall performance management approach for a local authority. It is used to measure progress towards achieving its goals, it calibrates conformance to policies, and assesses the performance of processes, systems, facilities and equipment. Without it the local authority simply does not know what it is doing. And therefore neither does the manager.

There are two main ingredients to the achievement of good performance measurement: a balanced range of measures and ownership of the ways of measuring performance.

The purpose of performance measurement is directly or indirectly to drive behavioural change. It is important to influence behaviour to change performance measures in the directions identified as 'positive'. To achieve these objectives, the organization must ensure that those being measured are aware of the balance of measures and that moving the measures in the positive direction will contribute to achievement of the organizational aims.

(Stainer and Heap, 1996)

In the long term, performance measures must be regarded as a part of our balanced approach to performance management in terms of the new performance management framework.

PERFORMANCE MEASURES

Performance measures have to be used to quantify objectives and to assess achievement. They are used in all aspects of the planning process, as well as for setting individual, team, service-wide and area objectives.

It is useful to distinguish the term 'performance measures' from 'performance indicators' and 'performance standards'. The following is taken from *People and Performance* (LGMB, 1993a):

Performance measure:
Purpose – give an index of achievement; judgement aid to consistency and fairness.
Relation to accountabilities – measure progress to (overall) end results.
Principles – distinguish units of measurement, eg, numbers, money, from measures of effectiveness and efficiency.
Efficiency – relationship of inputs to outputs, eg, unit costs, utilization, labour and productivity.
Trends – use for setting and assessing effectiveness, eg, standards, estimates, forecasts.
Effectiveness – relation of end result to a base using comparisons with, for example, standards, estimates, forecasts, external practice.

Units of measurement:
Money; measures of effectiveness include:
 maximizing income;
 minimizing expenditure;
 improving rates of return;
 comparisons with elsewhere.
Time; measures performance against:
 timetable or programme;
 amount of backlog;
 duration of 'temporary situation'.
Reaction; how others see you including:
 rating by customer, observer or assessor;
 appraisal through enquiry or report;
 comments in talk, correspondence and media;
 incidents of problems or disputes.

Effects; measures results including:
    change in behaviour;
    proportion of take up of service;
    completion of work;
    attainment of standard.

(Cambridgeshire County Council)

Performance measures range from very subjective to objective, and are descriptive. The following is a checklist for performance measures, which you may find useful.

– must relate to achievement not effort;
– must be objective and observable;
– the most objective measures are quantifiable;
– results must apply to the job holder's work;
– data must be available for measures;
– several measures can apply together;
– subjective measures should be rationalized;
– select the best measures;
– use or adapt existing measures wherever possible.

(Royal Borough of Kensington and Chelsea)

Performance standards

The performance standard is the agreed performance that is to be achieved. If a performance measure is the number of enquiries dealt with per hour, the performance standard is x enquiries per assistant per hour. The aim of standards is to assist in setting desired levels of performance, which are appraised to determine actual achievements and then form the basis for further improvement. Standards can be set for each measurable aspect of performance, and can be used to demonstrate economy, efficiency and effectiveness. They may be explicit – 5 per cent of return on capital, or implicit – acceptable rate of errors in a process.

Leading-edge managers working in the new local government context will need to reflect a high degree of social values to do with equality of opportunity and access. This removes the measurement of performance from the straightforwardly technical. For example, a library can double the number of books taken out from it, and technically double its performance. However, they could achieve this by persuading everyone who already comes in to the library to take out twice as many books as before. If the local authority has the aim of increasing the number of people who use their library then they have to try and attract different people into their library, and change from a technical performance measure.

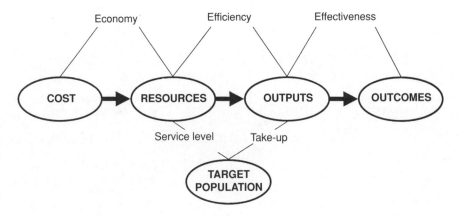

Figure 7.1 *Audit Commission performance review*

The Audit Commission has found it useful to conceptualize the process of measuring performance as illustrated in Figure 7.1 (and demonstrated in the case study below). This is a familiar process for local government managers: it distinguishes costs, resources provided, outputs and outcomes. While outputs measure the use made of resources, outcomes reflect the ultimate value or benefit of a service to its users.

The most difficult aspect of this whole model is measuring outcomes or the effectiveness of the service. Figure 7.2 is an outline model showing the key steps in designing a performance measurement system.

CASE STUDY: 1000 PERFORMANCE INDICATORS

REDDITCH BOROUGH COUNCIL

Redditch Borough Council defines the objectives of its performance review system as being: 'to measure council services objectively through a set of numerical indicators and relate these to a set of policy objectives and core values laid down by members'. The system covers all the council's activities and integrates corporate, service and individual performance targeting and assessment.

About 1000 performance indicators (PIs) have been identified at corporate and service level, including 'satisfaction quotients' obtained from the analysis of periodic questionnaires issued to a panel of over 500 local residents. A much smaller number of key indicators has been selected to enable members to focus on the more strategic aspects of each service. These include the Audit Commission's statutory PIs.

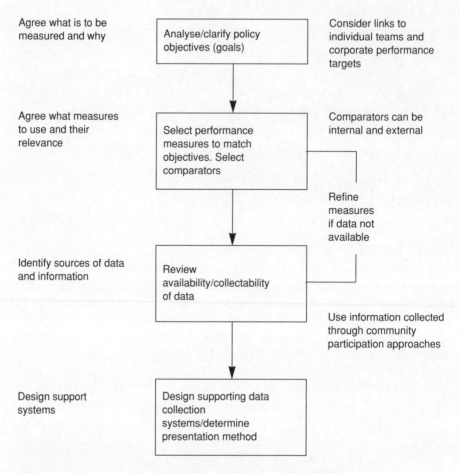

Agree what is to be measured and why

Analyse/clarify policy objectives (goals)

Consider links to individual teams and corporate performance targets

Agree what measures to use and their relevance

Select performance measures to match objectives. Select comparators

Comparators can be internal and external

Refine measures if data not available

Identify sources of data and information

Review availability/collectability of data

Use information collected through community participation approaches

Design support systems

Design supporting data collection systems/determine presentation method

Figure 7.2 *Key steps in designing a performance measurement system (adapted from Jackson and Palmer, 1994)*

The system is set in the context of a statement of the council's 10 corporate core values and objectives, which have been widely publicized, internally and externally. For each service there is a set of:

- Policy objectives – which are subject to review, but may remain relevant for a period of years.
- Annual key tasks – specific projects or achievements to be completed by set dates. A lead officer is designated for each key task, so providing a link to the tasks and targets for individual managers.
- Targeted performance indicators – both for the key tasks and for the costs and quality of the service as a whole. These performance

indicators are also reflected in the performance appraisal process for individual employees.

There is a strong emphasis on quantifiable indicators, together with a distinction between indicators of service activity or demand (for example the size of the housing waiting list) and indicators of service performance (such as the rate at which people are re-housed from the list). The system focuses on the latter, as volumes of demand are not within the authority's control.

In an explanatory document for members, managers and staff the emphasis on numerical indicators is explained thus:

If it is not possible to express an indicator in numeric terms, it is not possible to set targets. Performance review is about numerical analysis, though the numeric expression of the qualitative aspects of services (such as customer satisfaction) requires a more imaginative approach. If a service cannot be quantified at the point of delivery, then service outcomes can be quantified by measuring user satisfaction.

In selecting each indicator the authority applies five tests:

1. Is it relevant as a useful guide to efficiency and effectiveness of the service?
2. Is it measurable and are any new information systems necessary to produce the required data?
3. Is the indicator 'pure' so that it really measures what it seems to indicate?
4. Is the target realistic, while still aiming to stretch and improve the service?
5. Does it reflect the authority's core values and policy objectives?

(Audit Commission, 1997)

Some problems with PIs

PIs are important and must be treated with caution. The demands of the best value regime and the context of new local government mean that more emphasis will be placed on performance. Therefore the need to avoid some of the following pitfalls becomes essential:

- Efficiency rather than effectiveness – PIs focus on inputs more than outputs and outcomes. They concentrate on the input of resources to various levels of activity, but focus much less on outcome.

- Comparing like with like – PIs are wrongly used to make inappropriate comparisons for different service areas and indeed with other local authorities which have differing needs, demands and resource characteristics. Furthermore, the way in which the services are produced or delivered in each of the councils may be very different.
- Inaccurate data – data may be suspect for a number of reasons, including the delays associated with collation and the availability of the information in the right form.

 Task 7.2

Do the results of your performance measures feed into other performance management systems, including the budgetary process and staff development?

SUSTAINABILITY INDICATORS

Chapter 28 of Agenda 21 arising from the Rio summit in 1995 calls upon local authorities to develop actions plans for sustainable development at a local level. It states that: 'As the level of government closest to the people, local authorities play a vital role in educating, mobilizing and responding to the public to promote sustainable development.' By 1996, most local authorities in each country were to have undertaken a consultative process with their populations and achieved a consensus on a local Agenda 21 for the community. Since then much work has been undertaken by local authorities and their communities.

There has been a wide range of approaches and attitudes to Agenda 21. Some local authorities see it entirely as an environmental issue; others see it as an overarching issue to do with not only the local authority's environmental strategies but also economic, transport, educational and social issues and so on. The notion of sustainable indicators is an extremely challenging one as the issues are complex, cutting across a wide range of policy issues inside and outside the local authority, involving agencies at a national, regional and local levels. Transposed onto contemporary approaches to best value, issues of sustainability can become even more complex.

The new agenda for sustainable development is set out in the Local Government Management Board's document, *A Framework for Sustainability* (LGMB, 1993b). It emphasizes that sustainability is not identical to environmental protection. Sustainable development holds out a positive vision of a better world, both environmentally and in terms of the quality of human life. The challenge is to secure the social vision and the political responsibility to do it. New local government is about sustainable development because it is about adding value, about joined-up thinking and most of all it is citizen-centred.

New local government, in building its relationships with citizens, will take this on board as a challenge in terms of its civic leadership responsibilities. For this reason I have included a section in this chapter on sustainability and sustainable indicators, as they should form part of a local authority's overall performance management approach.

Achieving a workable definition of sustainability proved a difficult challenge for 67 experts from 15 countries at a conference initiated by the United Nations University in June 1992. Lists of sustainability characteristics were created. However, the outcome of the exercise emphasized that sustainability parameters change depending on the scale, from macro to micro regions. Local authority programmes attempt to explore and define what is meant by sustainable development at a local level, so that it makes sense to link the development of sustainable development indicators not only to the local Agenda 21 programme, but also to other policy planning and management systems of the local authority.

Sustainability indicator methodology is still in an embryonic stage. There is much theory evolving on the difference between sustainability indicators and environmental, social and economic indicators. Translating the theory into practice is acknowledged to be a process fraught with difficulties. The inadequate information base and definitions that are too vague to be a reliable guide to policy making are just two of the important reasons. From a local authority perspective there is a clear call for indicators that are simple and readily available. New local government will need to find ways of at least identifying a small range of performance indicators at a strategic level that are measurable and capable of being cascaded down into other levels of the organization's activities. Local authorities believe that as a part of their civic leadership role they have a responsibility for helping to improve the quality of life of their citizens, so they must work towards sustainability indicators.

Examples of sustainability indicators that relate to two particular themes, along with comments, are given in Tables 7.1 and 7.2, which come from the sustainability research project undertaken by local Agenda 21 UK.

Geographical information systems

Local authorities need to organize their information in a variety of ways. Usually it will cover the whole local authority as well as the specific unit of service. Increasingly, local authorities have decentralized their service delivery into smaller localities, so they need to map the localities within their boundaries.

Table 7.1 *Example of sustainability indicators (1)*

People live without fear of personal violence from crime or persecution because of their personal beliefs, race, gender or sexuality.	
Ref Indicator	**Comment**
1 Percentage of population feeling safe to go out at night.	A subjective but valuable indicator of freedom. Contributes to overall public perceptions of local quality of life.
2 Violent crimes/1000	Audit Commission indicator.
3 Burglaries/1000	Audit Commission indicator.
4 Annual increase in cost of property insurance (household, business).	Increases in premiums would reflect growing problems (actual and perceived).
5 Number of reported racially motivated assaults.	Despite problems of measurement a vital indicator of community relations.
6 Number of reported rapes/indecent assaults.	Justice is a crucial equity issue for sustainability but there are problems with measurement. Public safety is generally regarded as measurable.
7 Numbers of tribunal cases for discrimination/harassment.	This could indicate good industrial/ community relations (but might mask out-of-court settlements or cases not proceeded with).

Geographical information systems (GIS) technology is still relatively new in local government and it is most definitely under-utilized. Too often small groups of 'techies' experiment with the technology, but do not share or apply it to other relevant service areas.

GIS systems have the potential of giving on-line data to operational staff on what services are being provided, where and at what level, comparing one neighbourhood or ward with another. In this way GIS systems can allow managers to compare performance.

BENCHMARKING – THE ESSENTIAL TOOL

Performance management involves a wide range of comparisons, either of the same services over different periods, or more likely of different services. Surveys in the public and private sectors have demonstrated that over recent years the most significant tool being used to measure performance and transform organizations is benchmarking. The best value regime has led to local government using it as a tool. It is incredibly appropriate as benchmarking can be used flexibly at all levels within an organization. It can be used to compare performance inside and outside the organization, across sectors and across

Table 7.2 *Example of sustainability indicators (2)*

Everyone has access to the skills, knowledge and information needed to enable them to play a full part in society.	
Ref Indicator	**Comment**
1 Children under 5 in nursery/pre-school as a percentage of total.	Audit Commission indicator.
2 Pupil/teacher ratio.	Basic measure of quality of education.
3 Percentage of adult population in full/part time education or training (including evening classes).	Measurement could address the split between higher education students, unemployed on training courses, and 'traditional' adult education. Indicator could be skewed by presence of universities.
4 Percentage of 18–21 year olds in further/higher education or training.	The same comment as above is applicable.
5 Percentage of schools which have undertaken environmental education programmes, or in-service training (INSET) in the last two academic years.	Commitment to addressing environmental issues through local schools.
6 Publication of local environmental strategy, state of the environment report, etc.,	Easily understood; does this lead to measurable action rather than simply good OR?

different types of services. In Chapter 8 we will look at the Business Excellence Model as a framework for benchmarking and its contribution to improving performance. In this chapter we will focus on what benchmarking is, the process for benchmarking and some of the pitfalls.

Definitions of benchmarking

There are many definitions of benchmarking, including the following:

> The process of identifying and understanding and adapting outstanding practices from within the same organization or from other businesses to help improve performance.
>
> (Sara Cooke, the Stairway Consultancy)

> A standard against which something can be measured. A survey mark of a previously determined position used as a reference point.
>
> (A dictionary definition)

A systematic approach to business improvement where best practice is sought and implemented to improve process beyond the benchmark performance.

(Department of Trade and Industry, 1995)

Benchmarking is a rational, disciplined approach to continuous improvement which helps identify, compare and emulate best practice wherever it occurs.

(Codling, 1992)

We can see from this range of definitions that there are a number of common themes, including measurement, analysis of internal processes, comparison with others inside and outside the organization, and continuous improvement. Whatever your definition of benchmarking it will be important to build ownership of it and to communicate it to those who will be involved in the process.

The process for benchmarking

There are five types of processes for benchmarking:

1. Internal benchmarks: an internal unit comparing performance with another.
2. Competitive benchmarks: direct comparison with competitors. In many cases information will be commercially sensitive.
3. Functional benchmarks: comparisons with organizations in different, non-competing production or service sectors, with similar core operations.
4. Generic benchmarks: comparing identical functions irrespective of the business.
5. Customer benchmarks: comparing performance with customer expectations.

The benefits of benchmarking include:

● the establishment of performance goals,
● accelerating change,
● improving processes and eventually service quality,
● bringing some reality into the organization in terms of how well they are doing.

There are six key stages in the benchmarking process:

1. Identifying and understanding the processes you adopt.
2. Identifying and agreeing what and who to benchmark.

3. Data collection.
4. Data analysis and identification of performance gaps.
5. Planning improvements and identifying key actions.
6. Evaluation.

CASE STUDY: BENCHMARKING CENTRAL AREA ACCOMMODATION

COVENTRY CITY COUNCIL

Coventry City Council's Department for Personnel and Information Management has overall responsibility for the management of central area accommodation used by the City Council. This comprises 12 buildings and covers 29 000 square metres of office accommodation.

As part of the 1997/98 accommodation business plan, one of the key objectives was to carry out a central area accommodation review that takes into account both corporate and departmental requirements for the next two years, and provides benchmark data on the current efficiency of accommodation. The team identified two sets of data on which benchmarking could be collated:

1. The average charge per square metre of central area accommodation used.
2. The average amount of accommodation per person available, including office space, support areas (ie rest/meeting rooms) and storage space.

The Central Accommodation Services Manager has for each of the 12 buildings identified the different costs that constitute the overall charges to departments (rent, rates, service charges, heating, etc). The fully inclusive charge averaged out for the authority is then compared to the rents charged for equivalent buildings in Coventry city centre, which are marketed in a quarterly local publication entitled *Land & Property Guide*. A key difficulty in benchmarking these costs is that private landlords will offer peppercorn rents for initial periods of the lease, with a view to increasing costs over the period of the lease. This has to be averaged out to get a full comparison of the rents of the 12 buildings used.

During 1997 the team undertook a benchmarking exercise to determine the effectiveness of the use of central area accommodation by Coventry City Council as compared to national data. The survey of 4000 public and private sector organizations in the UK, conducted by Gerald Eve, provided benchmarking data for the Royal Institute of Chartered Surveyors. The team used this data to undertake Coventry's benchmarking exercise.

The team invested in a Computer Aided Facilities Management package (CAFM), which was used to record the space available and the number of staff in each central location. The development of this database provided local information to benchmark against national data.

Results of the survey

The Royal Institute of Chartered Surveyors' benchmark is 16 square metres per person, inclusive of actual office space used by staff, support space and storage space in use by a department in a typical administrative building. The average figure for Coventry City Council's use of central area accommodation is 12.81 square metres, which is 23 per cent below the national benchmark. Similarly, the cost per person to occupy space in the city centre is averaged at £1600 per annum, with a national average of £2300 per annum.

Common pitfalls

Some of the common pitfalls – and reasons for failure – in undertaking benchmarking activities are:

- poor planning;
- the chosen area for benchmarking lacks relevance to overall priorities;
- lack of understanding of the approach;
- no clear leader or ownership of the programme;
- the relevance to citizens and customers is not taken into account;
- lack of involvement of staff concerned with the processes being benchmarked.

 Task 7.3

What area of your service would you like to benchmark? Why? How would you take into consideration the views of service users? Consider how you can build ownership for undertaking such a project.

In Tower Hamlets they are using the benchmarking approach as a starting point for the development of a best value regime. Benchmarking is seen as a tool that will be used to develop techniques for giving feedback to local residents in community consultation aspects of the planned regime.

Tower Hamlets is a member of a benchmarking network of local authorities, sharing information on good practice. The network members participate in the process of benchmarking and analyse studies to identify performance levels and good practice for both immediate and future needs. Tower Hamlets resources each study and decides on the scope of each project. Projects are pulled together in agreed work programmes. Each member of the network agrees activities they wish to participate in. Authorities may select as many studies as they wish, although they are asked to select a third of the total studies. In return for participation each authority receives a copy of each study which includes completed copies of the data analysis for the exercise.

Process benchmarking is used widely by the local authorities. The aim of process benchmarking is first to look in detail at how one provides a service, analysing the processes used and identifying delays and problems. The next stage is to identify a good practice site or 'benchmarking partner', through the provision of a performance and process questionnaire. An analysis of the processes of the benchmarking partner is then carried out, to identify the good practice. Tower Hamlets take this a stage further, by bringing together all interested authorities to discuss the findings, looking to endorse the good practice and find further improvements to the process.

Local government services are generally very broad, and it is therefore unlikely that one would find all the good ideas in one authority. Experience has shown that it is more likely to come from a range of different authorities. The technique can be applied in any situation, but is best used for process-driven services such as housing benefits.

This benchmarking technique fits with best value requirements, through learning from good practice. The establishment of performance indicator outcomes enables future performance to be monitored and built into service improvement plans.

Critical to the success of this technique is that the study is owned by the service providers, including all staff being involved in the development of their service. It is also critical that the cost implications of service delivery choices are fully explored. Without these aspects, the ownership of outcomes becomes difficult, hampering the introduction of service improvements and the ability to measure value for money efficiencies.

The use of process benchmarking complements a range of other techniques, from performance review to total quality management and the Business Excellence Model.

 Task 7.4

Identify a range of services in your authority that would be suitable for process benchmarking. Choose one of these and brainstorm the steps involved.

CASE STUDY: BENCHMARKING SERVICES FOR UNDER-8S, LONDON BOROUGH OF TOWER HAMLETS

A study has been completed on the services for under-8s. This concerned applications and referrals to social services for places in day centres. The aim of the study was to consider the methods used to process an application, through to a place being allocated.

FIRST STEPS

The first step in the study was to carry out an overview interview with the principal officer for the under-8s service. The aim of this interview was to identify the general framework of the service, its constraints and boundaries, and to agree the service criteria and any particular problems the service faced in Tower Hamlets.

This discussion established the framework of performance and the process questionnaire that would be sent to participating authorities. The process questionnaire was developed and piloted with the principal officer and other staff. A process map of the high-level processes involved in the provision of the service was also produced, setting out the key functions. The questionnaire gathers information relevant to the service such as the number of requests received, the number of places available, whether alternatives were available and the budget for the year.

The aim of the questionnaire was to identify an authority that provided a service at a level of efficiency and cost which Tower Hamlets would wish to emulate. It is not normally possible to agree the concept of 'best service' due to the individuality of each local authority and its specific priorities. However, the approach identified as the 'best for us' would bring maximum benefits to Tower Hamlets, while also bringing good practice outcomes to benefit all participants.

DETAILED ANALYSIS

While the questionnaires were being completed by participating authorities, a more detailed analysis was carried out on Tower Hamlets' service. This included interviews with administrative staff responsible for the allocation of places at children's and family centres. This resulted in the production of 'process maps', a form of process flow analysis. These map out the process flow of information from the initial enquiry or referral onwards. This enabled a number of service improvements to be made at this stage, by examining how and why things are done and bringing ideas and identifying solutions to problems.

When the completed questionnaires were returned from participating authorities a 'benchmarking partner' was selected. This 'best for us' partner appeared to process applications more quickly, although the number of applications received were of a similar magnitude to Tower Hamlets.

SITE VISIT

A site visit was arranged to discuss the process within the partner authority. This visit identified the use of joint panels to allocate places at centres and to allocate childminding subsidy. The joint panels made decisions on the applications received and the attendance of applicants at the interview with the child present. Additional efficiencies identified included the effective use of translation services, which overcame the problem of application forms for those who had difficulty with written English. This attempted to ensure that those most in need had access to the service. Additionally, a panel did not sit to allocate places; instead, allocations were made on a priority basis, as soon as possible. Once the visit was completed, the processes were mapped out to mirror the functions of Tower Hamlets.

At this stage, there was a need to revisit the Tower Hamlets process, to look at the provision of childminding subsidy within the service, and for the procedures to be mapped out accordingly.

FINAL STAGE

The final stage of the study was to invite those authorities that completed a questionnaire to meet and discuss the findings. Four London boroughs met for half a day, and the outcomes formed the basis of the published report. Improvements at the club meeting included having peripatetic staff available to carry out home visits for interviews.

REPORT TO COMMITTEE

A committee report was prepared, encompassing the findings of the study and the potential improvements available to the service. The findings were agreed and a working party set up within the service to bring about the changes. These included the use of interviews, thus reducing the number of panels; early allocations; and the use of translators in place of application forms for those who could not write English.

OUTCOMES

One of the aims of the study was to provide a unified approach to services for the under-8s. This has been achieved in part, through the development of a unified approach to applications, although the available budget for subsidy limits the scope for this development.

Benchmarking is an important process for local government. It provides detailed performance information on different services from other local authorities. Leading-edge managers should recognize that this process helps them learn how to improve their services and because it means that local authorities learn from each other, the manager will have made some important cooperative contacts in other local authorities. Local authorities often don't learn from each other as much as they might, so all contact between managers in different authorities is to be cherished. This reflects a key attribute of leading-edge managers: the ability to network inside and outside the organization.

SUMMARY

Many of the previous chapters outline the different levels and components of a performance management system. The manager needs to recognize that none of these can work without the relevant information that measures performance. However, performance will be measured through a variety of different mechanisms that generate different data. It is important that the leading-edge manager is on top of them.

REFERENCES

Audit Commission (1997) *Paying the Piper Calling the Tune – People, Pay and Performance in Local Government*, Audit Commission, London.

Jackson, P and Palmer, B (1994) *First Steps in Measuring Performance in the Public Sector*, Public Finance Foundation, London.

LGMB (1993a) *People and Performance*, LGMB, London.

LGMB (1993b) A Framework for Sustainability, LGMB, London.

Stainer, A and Heap, J (1996) 'Performance management. A management service perspective', *Management Service Journal*, July.

Wedgewood Oppenheimer, F (1996) *Managing Information in Local Government*, Inlogov, London.

The shape of learning organizations and performance

This chapter is concerned with organizational performance. So far we have discussed two of the quadrants of the new performance management framework outlined in Chapter 3. In quadrant one, civic leadership and democracy, we discovered aspects to do with citizens and performance and political management. Quadrant two on strategic management was concerned with macro performance, and the contribution of information and measuring performance. Quadrant three is about results obtained by people and the first of two arenas within this quadrant is organizational performance.

In this chapter we will explore how leading-edge managers can improve performance management capability through the principles of the learning organization. We will see how they can create 'organizations where people continually expand their capability to create the results they truly desire' (Senge, 1990).

Let us examine the word 'organization'. It has at least two common everyday meanings: first, the collection of people who constitute some kind of group, network or structure, and, second, a way of ordering a task, process or work and how it is undertaken. Next generation management will be less concerned with formal structures, and more with how people work as individuals and in a team. In particular they will be concerned as to how learning is undertaken and how it contributes to better performance.

Drucker and others have talked a lot about how organizations of the future would have fewer levels of management. This is now becoming much more typical of local government. Drucker also talks about future organizations as being knowledge-based, empowered and self-directing. Traditional command and control models will be irrelevant. In those organizations where work is currently carried out within departments or functions, Drucker suggests that tomorrow the functions of businesses will be carried out by a wide range of ad hoc 'task focused teams' (Drucker,1998).

Drucker's vision of the future organization can be seen in its embryonic stage within local government today. Local authorities which have already dispensed with departments and directorates and have de-layered the organization begin to form cross-service and inter-agency teams to work on specific services or initiatives. For example, in the 1990s local authorities were expected to compete for very specific funds such as the Single Regeneration Budget. The only way a local authority could successfully bid for monies that would be awarded to genuinely corporate projects was to organize themselves to build a bid that cut across departments. Successful bids generally reflected a number of services within the local authority and a wide range of external organizations from other public, private and community interests that are brought together to form a vision, strategies and action plans to achieve specific objectives, for example the regeneration of a neighbourhood.

Clearly there is a huge challenge here for next generation management. This challenge is about managing a diverse organization consisting of a wide range of 'task focused teams', and monitoring their performance. It is imperative to link their performance to the overall priorities and objectives of the local authority and of other agencies too.

THE LEARNING ORGANIZATION

The ways of working described above will require next generation management to take on board fully the principles of the learning organization. As rigid organizational hierarchies are disappearing, so also are traditional processes of operational control. The focus of the learning organization here is to harness the full energy, capabilities and competencies of the people who work within the local authority to meet the needs and demands of citizens now and in the future. This of course implies that the local authority has a vision of what the future might look like, and in moving towards the future the local authority will value the core competencies of the organization and the creativity of the people who work for it. A popular definition of a learning organization is used by Pedler (1992): 'An organization which facilitates the learning of all of its members and continuously transforms itself'.

The 'learning organization' is not the same as 'organizational learning', which is about the sum of all of the learning that takes place in an organization and how this impacts on the organization's performance. It would include personnel strategies, training and development, and the acquisition of new skills and knowledge. The learning organization is a rather more complex concept since it encompasses the capacity of the organization to transform itself for its future needs and expectations.

The term 'learning organization' has been in vogue for quite some time. However, it has not been practised fully within the local government environment. Next generation management will need to truly adopt the principles of the learning organization to work in different ways and to take on continuous change and ensure high performance. The learning organization means Councils need to learn and encourage learning in the people that work for us inside and outside the organization.

The shape and culture of local authorities can facilitate and encourage learning, or act as an incredible barrier to it. Therefore achieving learning organization status may require structural and cultural change. It is hard to imagine that this change will not be radical in most local authorities. Learning values such as openness, questioning, willingness to discuss, testing out ideas, reflecting on actions, and sharing are important. Organic type organizations are more likely to be conducive to learning due to the freedom from hierarchical controls and the ability to network horizontally and vertically, leading to good communication.

Asking questions is an important aspect of the learning organization and best value principles as it helps managers to understand and test out ideas. When managers begin a new appointment it is an ideal opportunity to gather members of staff together and ask a whole band of questions to do with the service area, its relationships with customers and other parts of the organization, and so on. In this way one can help to tease out any underlying causes of poor performance, poor morale and esteem. The Japanese are excellent at sending their local government managers around the world to work with other local authorities, to ask questions about what is done, how it is done and why. They are required to analyse situations and reflect on them in terms of their own working environment.

Leading-edge managers will put aside time for their people to question, think and learn from inside and outside the Council.

CASE STUDY: REAL CHANGE LEADERS (RCL) PROGRAMME

The RCL is an improvement process that uses Team Learning™ to equip teams to respond effectively and creatively to rapid change. It was devised by the organizational learning group at the LGMB.

The RCL programme consists of the Learning Lab, which includes 15 optional modules, and is based on the application of Peter Senge's ideas in *The Fifth Discipline*. It has been extensively tested in both the private and public sectors, internationally.

The Learning Lab introduces participants to the skills and techniques embodied in Senge's five disciplines:

1. Mental models – understanding ourselves and each other, finding new ways of communicating honestly and openly to have different, more constructive conversations.
2. Systems thinking – avoiding making damaging 'quick fixes'.
3. Team learning – learning together to reinforce the learning and provide power to change.
4. Personal mastery – knowing what you want and how to achieve it.
5. Shared vision – focusing on the real work of the team.

The programme also includes a process for business planning which harnesses the creativity of the group to improve service delivery.

The RCL Learning Lab takes place in the team's work environment, in real time, using real work issues. It consists of a workbook, videos and group activities, supported by a coach who helps the participating team through the programme. It takes from 20 to 24 hours for a team to complete the Learning Lab.

The RCL programme is an innovative example of how leading-edge managers can come together and implement the principles of the learning organization in live situations.

The causes of success and failure

Next generation management will not just be interested in the causes and analysis of failure and implementing the lessons that can be learnt, nor with reading books on best practice and trying to use it in their own situation. Rather, they will be concerned with analysing the causes of success and replicating these behaviours in the new local government environment. In this way leading-edge managers are questioning and working through why issues have occurred, reflecting on them and relating them to their own personal environments.

Learning styles

People have different learning styles and preferences, although many can adapt to a wide range of learning styles. Leading-edge managers should identify the learning preferences of their people, ensuring that wherever possible learning activities can be optimized by individuals and groups contributing to the higher levels of performance we are seeking. In Chapter 2 we discussed the importance of staff development and identifying relevant development and training opportunities. Here we can see it is just as important that the development opportunity is conducive to the individual's preferred learning style.

What is a learning Council like?

A learning Council is one that:

- encourages all levels in the organization to learn on and off the job to develop their capability;
- extends the learning culture to citizens, communities, and stakeholders;
- regards the intellectual capital of its people as a primary strength in terms of high performance in meeting citizens needs;
- has a willingness to transform the way it works, its shape and relation-ships;
- has a high level of integrity, is open and honest about what it has or has not achieved;
- has a blame-free culture;
- continuously facilitates the learning of all its people;
- transforms itself to meet its citizens' needs;
- recognizes that there is no single model of a learning organization;
- is characterized by *how* the council does things, not *what* it does;
- is not a comfortable organization or easy place to work in.

The purpose of transformation as a central part of the learning organization is for it to reframe itself to meet the needs of citizens.

 Task 8.1

Consider a current problem within your organization. How is it being addressed? Is it being tackled in the context of a learning organization? Is learning encouraged? If not, what are the main blockages to learning?

ACTION LEARNING

Action learning concentrates on actual managerial issues raised in the learning group by individual group members and therefore has an immediate and practical applicability. It originated, according to Reg Evans who might justifiably be called the 'father' of action learning, during 'the nationalization of the British coal industry. It emerged that much less was known about how to run a pit than experts would admit to – particularly when they were overwhelmed by the political hurricane that struck their ancient culture' (Pedler *et al*, 1991).

Colliery managers found that to survive they had to work together on the practical problems they faced, admit their shortcomings and ignorance, and share whatever experience and expertise they had. A representative sample of 22 managers from pits all over England and Wales worked together over a three-year period to address the issues and problems they faced. They were supported by a team under a technical leader or a seconded manager and a number of graduate mining trainees. Managers identified a problem at their own mine, and explained to colleagues the possible origins of the problem, inviting ideas as to how it could be dealt with, reporting progress with possible readjustments, and evaluating.

Success in this very practical method of problem solving and learning led to other action learning sets being established on a local and international basis. Sometimes they were allied to a particular project, and had a life span concurrent with that of the project, but increasingly the job became the project, and groups had an extended life. Action learning-set members looked for practical solutions to the task. They explored the decision making processes behind that and the interplay between the human and technical side of difficulties. As Reg Evans makes clear, 'action learning demands not only self-disclosure of personal perception and objective but the translation of belief and opinion into practice'. Discussion generated in action learning sets must therefore have immediate applicability to the situation.

Action learning is a core element of the LGMB's Top Manager Programme which has been very successful in the late 1990s in training over 600 managers to meet the future challenges of local government.

The Local Government Management Network, a national organization concerned with the development and learning of senior managers within local government, formed a wide range of 'policy nets'. The policy nets themselves are in fact action learning sets of between 12 and 16 individual officers from around the country who come together to address a specific issue. They meet six times a year with a highly respected professional who facilitates their thinking, questioning and the solutions they put forward to meet their own individual and organizational challenges. The policy nets also form sub-groups to deal with common issues and e-mail networks to share information and of course meet when they wish without the facilitator. A number of the policy nets have organized joint meetings and meetings among sub-groups from different policy nets. This typifies how networked knowledge-based organizations will work in the future.

Bob Garratt, a colleague and international management consultant, identified four key elements of the action learning process (Garratt, 1990):

- a crucial organization problem;
- people willing to take risks to develop themselves and their organizations;
- authority to take action on the problem;
- a system for learning reflectively.

Issues are therefore real for the managers, and learning not dictated by academics, fashion or a top manager with a particular hobbyhorse. Learning comes from the turmoil which the problem is creating for the manager and the motivation to improve the situation. Trust and confidentiality are crucial components of the action learning-set process, and need to be established from the outset so that managers are completely open about the nature of the problem.

CASE STUDY: A NON-LOCAL GOVERNMENT ACTION LEARNING SET

A former chief executive joined an action learning set through Ashridge. In the set of five members, the other four were from the private sector. The first year they had a contract for four meetings per year, facilitated by an Ashridge consultant – 'you can't plunge into action learning without a facilitator'. The set is now in its twelfth year, unfacilitated (except by its own members), having met four, then three and currently twice a year. The pattern of meetings that has evolved includes an overnight stay, members meeting the previous evening for dinner and socializing, then working the following day from 8am to 1pm before departure. All group members have a 'slot', with the most urgent first, and time allocated accordingly. The group's task is to ask questions of the member presenting the issue, in order to enable him or her to come to their own solution. Issues presented are 'those which people can't solve by themselves' and are dominated by those to do with relationships, with dealing with specific tasks second.

'It's been the most powerful learning tool since being a chief executive' says a member who used it to learn how others were dealing with issues, particularly those from the private sector context, such as marketing and those having a commercial business approach. 'It was good to be with people I would never be in competition with'. Inevitably over the 12 years there were major changes for members in job and personal terms, and they could choose whether and how much to share with group members. 'I learnt about myself and how I came across to others – peers are good at judging how others see you and sensing what motivates you. They're good at helping you focus on your future – something you can't share with those you work with'.

(Source: LGMB, 1996.)

THE BUSINESS EXCELLENCE FRAMEWORK

Performance within the learning organization needs to be inspired, supported and nurtured in whatever ways can assist with transforming your organization into a high performance, modern local authority. Although there is limited use of the Business Excellence Framework within local government it does provide a framework for us to adapt some of the key features of next generation management.

Over recent years Xerox has won the European Foundation for Quality Management's award several times. This is no mean feat. I have spent a number of days working with senior directors and managers within the Xerox organization and found that they have adapted the model to reflect the language and use within their own company, enabling them to highlight different aspects. Next generation management can do the same. A number of people, including Professor Colin Talbot of Cardiff University, continue to develop a Public Service Excellence Model.

European Foundation for Quality Management (EFQM)

The Business Excellence Framework or European Quality Model was developed from ideas about 'stakeholding', 'total quality' and 'benchmarking' in the private sector. The concept of the model was developed by Malcolm Baldridge in the USA and became the basis of their National Quality Awards in 1987, followed by the European Quality Award in 1992 and the first UK Award for Business Excellence Awards in 1994. The European/UK model was developed through consensus among a wide range of corporate organizations.

The model, shown in Figure 8.1, is based on the importance of stakeholders (hence the inclusion of criteria relating to 'results' about staff, customers and 'impact on society') and total quality (hence the emphasis on both internal 'enabler' and external 'results'). It clearly draws on the 'continuous improvement' schools of thought. Providing a common framework and criteria against which to measure any organization, it is helpful for benchmarking a local authority as a whole and in specific areas of activity. Given the model was created in the private sector, local authorities need to be particularly aware of the following:

- the language used, especially terms such as 'customer' and 'competitor' – notions of citizenship and citizens and service users need to be integrated into the model;
- a need for interpretation of specific criteria in the model, especially 'business results' and 'impact on society' (in using the model I have replaced the latter with 'social justice values');

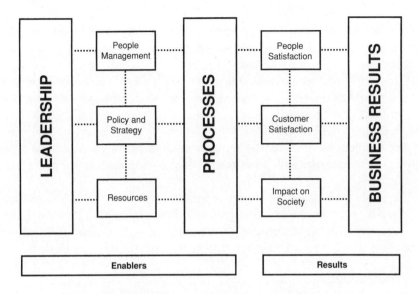

Figure 8.1 *The Business Excellence Model*

- applying the model to small areas of activity, where there are issues to do with economies of scale and the time and energy put into them.

The model has been used in the public sector in central and local government, the NHS and other public bodies. A more systematic attempt has been by the Civil Service Executive Agencies, which started with a pilot project in 1996 involving 30 agencies, and a further project which began in 1997 involving 45 agencies (Talbot, 1997). The Civil Service College is developing a database of results from over 70 agencies covering 300 000 staff and 21 other public bodies. The evaluation of the use of the Business Excellence Model within the Civil Service concluded that although the model worked overall, there were some difficulties in defining and weighting the importance of customers, competitors and impacts on society.

Why a Public Service Excellence Model?

Talbot argues that the advantages of a model-based approach are obvious. If well designed it allows for comparisons across diverse organizations. However, there are obvious weaknesses – the more generic the model the more likely it is to be inappropriate for any individual organization.

The overall structure and weighting of the Business Excellence Model gives great importance to competition. Although this was seen as a major disadvantage some years ago, it is now viewed as a valuable challenge for local government, as the best value regime requires local authorities to become more competitive. The emphasis on customer satisfaction is still very relevant as new local government values customers as citizens and citizens as customers.

A key challenge for next generation management is to decide how best to use the model as a significant tool in their overall approach to creating a high performing, modern local authority. The need for inter-agency, cross-service working and neighbourhood working in new local government brings even greater challenges in terms of how to hold those responsible for service delivery accountable and how best to share approaches to performance management.

The Business Excellence Model is perhaps best used when it is re-framed for specific circumstances within each individual organization and set of organizations. Different elements of the model can be used at different times as necessary to complement other aspects of performance management.

CASE STUDY: LEARNING TO DEVELOP A COHERENT APPROACH

SOLIHULL METROPOLITAN BOROUGH COUNCIL

Solihull MBC has explored approaches to quality management since the early 1980s. This case study examines the succession of initiatives in the authority which have addressed issues of quality, performance and customer service.

Solihull has had an interest in customer care initiatives since the early 1980s. In the mid-1980s, there was a move to business planning and performance indicators in the authority. In 1986, the 'Customer First' initiative was launched, based on the firmly held views of the then leader of the Council, a local businessman, that private sector philosophies of customer service were also applicable in the public sector. This initiative was strongly backed by the then chief executive. In 1989, Solihull became the first Council to win a National Training Award for staff training, which focused on Customer First training for front-line staff. This initiative is now deeply embedded in the culture, with less cynicism than in many other local authorities.

From the early 1990s, emphasis was given to wider issues of quality management. In 1992 the Environmental Health and Trading Standards Department was the first in Britain to achieve registration to ISO 9000; nine months later, Education Catering also achieved registration, but no others have followed. Education Catering also obtained the Charter Mark.

In 1992, Solihull set out to achieve Investors in People status for the whole authority; in 1995 it became the first metropolitan authority to do so.

However, there have also been failed initiatives. A number of departments have sought Charter Marks during the early 1990s, with only one success. This had a dispiriting effect on the departments concerned, and has brought a degree of cynicism about the criteria being used by the Citizen's Charter Unit in Whitehall. Recently, Solihull reached the final shortlist of six for the SOLACE/PA Consulting 'Total Quality' Award. While this was hardly a failure in itself, the authority took to heart the feedback given by PA Consulting on why it had not gone on to win. In particular, it accepted the criticisms that there were no formal 'total quality' reviews, that there was no sense of 'where next?' and that there was a lack of overall direction on quality. To remedy this situation, the authority has decided to adopt the Business Excellence Model. This is expected to provide the comprehensive framework inside which the many individual initiatives can be refined and coordinated.

Total quality management cannot be a piecemeal approach. Solihull has been implementing some individual quality initiatives for ten years, and some of them have been very successful and become deeply embedded within the culture. Yet this has not been sufficient to guarantee that the overall culture would become quality-oriented. There is a need for constant renewal of quality initiatives but even more for a constant widening of their applications, within a framework that is acceptable to all departments. However gratifying success in certain quality competitions and awards may be, it is more important to focus on providing a coordinated structure and set of processes for quality management which will bring synergy to the individual initiatives.

(Source, LGMB, 1996).

FORM FOLLOWS FUNCTION AND CREATES CULTURE

The form or shape of the organization will inevitably influence its culture and how it works and performs.

Choosing the right form should depend on the nature of the service being provided, the culture of the organization or the way that the organization wants to work. The following are snapshots of the types of organizations that local government represents today and will represent in terms of next generation management.

Hierarchical

This is the traditional command and control organization, and is illustrated in Figure 8.2. Slow to change, this type of organization works well in stable environments. There is no reward for innovation or taking risks. This form of structure is not even old local government, it is *ancient* local government! New local government cannot work within such a structure as it cannot adapt quickly to environmental changes and is not conducive to being outward-looking and working on an inter-agency basis.

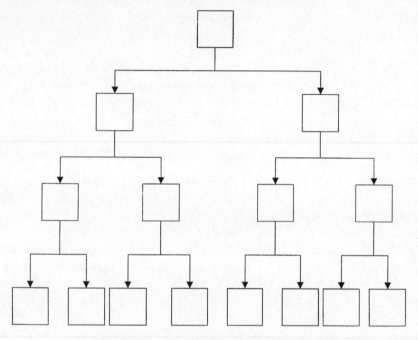

Figure 8.2   *The hierarchical organization*

Matrix

Over the last ten years or so, many local authorities have, in a response to changes in managerial thinking, removed a few layers of the organization. The hierarchy is basically overlain by a wide range of project teams with individuals from functional departments and managers from the centre (see Figure 8.3). In the early 1980s this way of working was seen to be successful as it brought together people from across the organization to manage issues and projects. However, very rarely were they about developing services and thinking through how best to deliver them. Matrix management had its limitations as managers found it increasingly difficult to have several people to report to, and the old hierarchical nature or culture came back into play. In some instances matrix working was implemented through necessity to meet environmental changes rather than to achieve more effective working and learning. Matrix working within the hierarchical organization makes it difficult for individuals to balance their priorities, loyalties and roles. A member of staff seconded to a project team will have to be loyal to both that team and to the hierarchical management structure he or she will return to at the end of the secondment.

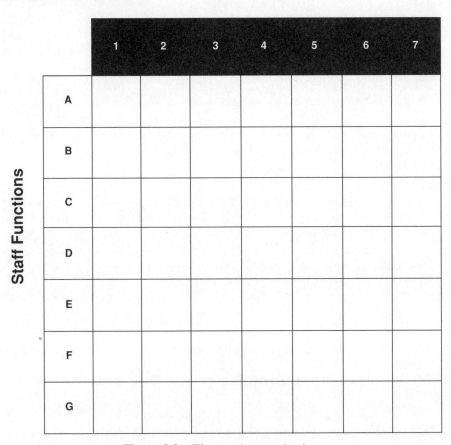

Figure 8.3   *The matrix organization*

CASE STUDY: DELAYERING IN THE 1990S
WYCOMBE DISTRICT COUNCIL

In the early 1990s Wycombe District Council had a programme of organizational delayering to create flatter departmental structures and to widen spans of managerial control and accountability. Delayering was one of the Council's responses to the challenges presented by compulsory competitive tendering and local government reorganization.

While the Council enthusiastically embraced the principles of performance management (it was the fourth local authority to be awarded Investors in People status), supporting organizational structures remained largely traditional. They have been characterized by quite extensive departmental hierarchies, with perhaps five or six layers of management separating chief officers from direct service providers. The Council began to regard 'tall' pyramidal structures as barriers to efficiency and effectiveness and contrary to its performance management culture.

Officers identified a number of unwelcome consequences arising from multiple layers of management. These included a bureaucratic decision making process which stifled innovation and impaired organizational responsiveness. With extensive hierarchies also came limited spans of management control. Officers felt that many jobs overlapped with others in a different tier, thus blurring lines of responsibility and accountability.

At the start of 1994, each department was asked to begin reviewing its structure and told that it was expected to have completed any re-organization within two years of starting the review. Officers used a proprietary job evaluation system to help them identify roles/responsibility overlaps and to determine scope for deleting posts and/or combining jobs. Guidelines recommended that departments tried to reduce their numbers of layers to four, by adopting the following model:

1. Chief officer: to provide strategic management and policy direction.
2. Head of service: to coordinate overall service provision.
3. Unit manager: to manage the operational delivery of specific services.
4. Front-line staff: to deliver services directly to the public.

This four-layer model was regarded by the Council as the optimum means of widening spans of control, increasing empowerment, improving cost-effectiveness and raising standards of service delivery.

Wycombe has gradually extended this approach throughout departments, rather than embarking on a rapid restructuring of the whole Council. The reduction in staffing achieved by such measures has helped the Council to contain payroll inflation to less than 1 per cent per year for the past three years.

Wycombe District Council's approach and openness is commendable. However, the concept of departments can still form barriers to effective inter-service working.

Cloverleaf

This form of organization, shown in Figure 8.4, is a development of the 'shamrock organization' put forward by Charles Handy (1989), described in detail later in the chapter.

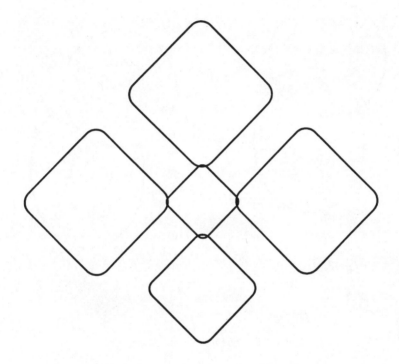

Figure 8.4 *The cloverleaf organization*

Networks

These are more loosely grouped networks of people and organizations that work together (see Figure 8.5). There is not necessarily a hierarchy here. When no hierarchy exists the networked organization has sub-groups of work teams that are particularly autonomous, quite possibly working with different values and visions. Teams are led by a controlling group or the individual who originates the initiative or project. People that work here are in business for themselves or work within other organizations and can be brought together at varying levels that undertake tasks. It is difficult to say where the network organization begins and finishes. Each mode of activity has many links inside and outside.

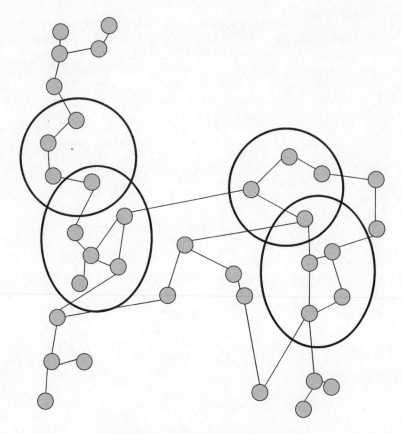

Figure 8.5 *The networked organization*

This clearly is not a form that will be conducive to local government. Principally this is because local government is accountable to elected representatives who form a political centre for the organization and will always be influenced by standards, procedures, government guidelines, and issues to do with probity, openness and transparency. That means inevitably that there will be some form of political and managerial centre. However, many of the characteristics of networked knowledge-based organizations can be transposed into local authorities that have dispensed with departments and directorates, have shortened hierarchies and have created learning cultures, fostering cross-service and inter-agency working with clear lines of accountability for performance.

In Chapter 9 the principles of holonic and fractal teams are discussed, giving us some ideas on how new local government can work in the above ways, harnessing energy, skill, talent and knowledge, while working with optimum flexibility to achieve performance targets.

Task 8.2

The structure and shape of your organization is more important than the way people work. The way services have to be delivered to meet citizens' needs should dictate what the shape of the organization should be. Do you agree?

THE SHAMROCK AND NEXT GENERATION MANAGEMENT

Local government is increasingly being judged on how well it delivers its responsibilities. Citizens' expectations are higher than ever before. There is a determination to see best value in all that we do when we are looking at how we create and deliver services. Unlike the private sector, local government has an imperative of ensuring that what we do is sustainable and reflects the values of social justice. The cost of sustainability issues and social justice has rarely been factored into performance indicators and the way in which local government works.

Next generation management will hold these values dearly in terms of how they meet the needs of citizens and shape organizations to facilitate and deliver. Management guru Charles Handy provides local government with an excellent description of the shape of organizations that can best reflect new local government: the shamrock organization. Many of us think of the shamrock as the Irish national emblem – a small clover-like plant with three leaves to each stem. Charles Handy uses the shamrock as an illustration of the three different groups of people within this type of organization. There is very little in terms of hierarchy. There is a core team of full-time professional staff essential to running the organization's core functions, and a range of different delivery mechanisms. The teams surrounding the organization or work groups contain staff who work in flexible ways: part-timers, self-employed, contracted staff, etc. This type of organization can deal very rapidly with the changing environment of local government and is particularly suited to dealing with time-limited projects and initiatives, which are so much a feature of today's local government.

In the UK I have seen little evidence of this type of organization within local government. However, in other parts of the world, including South Africa, I have seen a large metropolitan authority reduce its core to less than 25 professionals including the chief executive and support staff. The rest of the organization's functions are either sub-contracted or undertaken by work teams consisting of officers from a range of second-tier authorities. This, even in South Africa, is an exception. There is much research and learning to be undertaken into how this form of organization could possibly help us to work

149

better in the new local government context. Best value may provide some impetus for local authorities to investigate the cloverleaf form.

Below I take Handy's model and interpret it for the context of new local government and next generation management.

Leaf 1

This would consist of the strategic core of the local authority, including the chief executive, executive directors and a range of highly skilled professionals whose competencies are to do with leadership, influencing and negotiation, networking, innovation management, communication, performance management and ensuring a relevant interface with political management of the local authority and citizens. They would be concerned not only with issues to do with the strategic management of the organization, but also issues to do with the Council's civic leadership and governance role.

This group of workers will reflect the values of social justice, high quality services and good government. They will be networkers and have the capability to work at different levels inside and outside the organization. They will be few in number and therefore will be well paid and highly valued by the organization.

Leaf 2

This will consist of a wide range of different service delivery mechanisms including loose partnerships, joint ventures, arm's-length companies and sub-contracted work. We have seen over the last ten years an emergence of these ways of working which in the future will form real options for alternative delivery mechanisms for new local government. The challenge for new local government here will be how to hold such organizations accountable for their actions and performance.

In Chapter 6 we discussed alternative forms of service delivery and some of the ways in which stronger working relationships and accountability mechanisms could be put in place to ensure the performance of these organizations. There are implications here for managers and elected members. For managers it will mean different forms of employment contract and even working across sectors. It may even mean being employed by more than one organization. For elected members the key issue is how to ensure that these organizations are accountable. The transformation of current ways of working will take some time and it is not entirely certain that any more than half of local government services will be delivered in this way, as there are many services which are to do with addressing the major issues facing our society, to do with regulation and where markets have yet to emerge.

Leaf 2 reflects new local government operating in a highly competitive mixed economy of service provision. Such an organization will only succeed if it is genuinely open to competition from private companies. No local government organization can keep abreast of the innovations that are taking place in the service industry sector unless they are open to the private services sector. Competition therefore provides the local authority with an opportunity to learn from what is happening elsewhere.

Leaf 3

This is to do with the flexible labour force.

As the structure of society changes – more parents looking for flexible hours and weekend working to share child-care arrangements; more of our longer term unemployed looking for flexible working so that they can study or hold down several jobs at once; increasing numbers of older people wanting to work beyond 60 to supplement their pensions – the more popular leaf 3 of the Shamrock organization becomes.

The following ways of working will be on the agenda of every manager, as they can contribute to more flexible, effective and efficient ways of employing individuals while meeting the individual's personal and social needs and of course needs of the service user – our citizens:

- part-time with fixed or variable hours
- weekend or evening shifts
- zero-hour contracts
- annual hours or seasonably variable hours
- school term-time only employment
- fixed-term contracts or contracts for performance
- standby, supply or other temporary employment
- job sharing
- voluntary reduced work time
- career breaks and sabbaticals
- home-based and tele-working.

Examples of where these staff will be employed include libraries, schools, leisure facilities, grounds maintenance, and so on. These workers certainly cannot replace the majority of staff for the provision of most services. However, they will be a significant part of future working.

Challenges for leading-edge managers of managing a shamrock organization

It is vital to appreciate that the shamrock organization must be managed across all three leaves. This calls for a much greater degree of networking and coordination to ensure that the three different parts of the organization work together. Such a form of networking avoids the creation of unnecessary sub-groups associated with old ways of working.

The challenges of managing a shamrock organization in new local government can be summarized as:

- accountability for performance at different levels of the organization across a wide range of different service delivery mechanisms;
- synchronizing service planning with corporate priorities;
- building in community participation as a way of working for sub-contracted services;
- inequalities of pay within the different leaves;
- dealing with poor performance across a range of multi-faceted contracts for individuals, teams and other organizations;
- ensuring that the staff employed in the first leaf have the time and support to continually learn about and understand the changing nature of the organization; and trust, honesty and openness at the core of the organization.

CORE COMPETENCIES AND INTELLECTUAL CAPITAL

Core competencies

Another way of looking at the future shape and form of local authorities is through the idea of core competencies. Prahalad and Hamel's article on core competencies (1990) has influenced me to think about the core competencies and capabilities of local authorities. Here we are talking not of the individual's competence but the organization's competence. Much of the literature on core competencies is to do with the contribution to strategic management. Prahalad and Hamel propose a different approach, to supplement current strategic planning methodology. Current approaches to strategic planning are about understanding the external environment by looking outside and then inwards. A local authority might decide to begin with an external analysis of what competencies it needs to service its role in the local area, then perform an internal analysis.

Prahalad and Hamel advocate an inside-out process – an internal analysis of the organizational capability and then the external environment. Leading-edge local government managers will understand the need to analyse the capabilities of their local authorities, and to make informed judgements as to how these capabilities can contribute to delivering citizens' needs and expectations currently and in the future. In this way a local authority can decide what might best be done in-house and what needs to be done externally.

Examples of core competencies of local authorities that might be relevant for new local government include:

- the ability to use information technology to communicate with and involve citizens in decision making;
- a community-based approach to giving advice and information on benefits;
- flexible working arrangements;
- knowledge of service users' needs on an area, neighbourhood and even street-by-street basis;
- integrated document management processes for dealing with multiple enquiries such as housing benefit, Council Tax or the needs of individuals cutting across different service areas.

Prahalad and Hamel's notion of core competence is a conceptual tool for use within the private sector to undertake a more rigorous examination and exploitation of a firm's internal strengths. Next generation management will need to understand the local authority's core competencies – things that it does very well – and how these can be used to position services more competitively and to add even further value for citizens.

The identification of organizational core competencies at a service and team level can also help us understand how we can bring teams together and create even more value. We can create that value in terms of the priorities and targets we are pursuing to ensure that we contribute to more effective and efficient performance. The local authority's competencies will be to do with the skills and knowledge within the organization, whereas organizational capabilities will be to do with local authority's ability to exploit resources such as information technology capability, marketing capability, community participation capability. They are functionally based.

Next generation management will need to find ways of identifying the capabilities and competencies of staff and the organization to enable them to make decisions on how best to organize the delivery of services. High performance will only be achieved if it is based on the organization's current capabilities and competence.

Intellectual capital

There are many different perspectives on intellectual capital within the private sector, its relationships to behaviour, changing corporate language and links to the balanced score card approach (see Chapter 10). Next generation management is concerned with individuals within the learning organization. If we refer this back to our previous discussion on the future form and shape of local government, we will begin to understand that the intellectual capital of our staff is an important factor in the organization's capability and competencies, the positioning of the local authority and its businesses, and in turn its overall performance. Intellectual capital within the local government arena should be viewed as the knowledge, skills and experience of our people and their ability to transform this into innovations, relationships and networks for the benefit of citizens.

In earlier chapters we have discussed knowledge as a valuable resource. Auditing the organization's intellectual capital is therefore an important step in understanding the capability and competencies of local authorities. This audit should enable local authorities to make more informed decisions about a wide range of issues, including what they are good at doing, how they could improve where necessary, and where value can be added to service quality.

SUMMARY

In this chapter we have considered how the culture, values and shape of an organization can impact on overall performance. Just as importantly we have acknowledged the need to understand the organization's capability as well as that of its people, as the two are inextricably related.

In Chapter 9 we explore how different approaches to team working, while requiring different work practices, can contribute to creating a high performance, modern local authority.

REFERENCES

Drucker, P F (1998) 'The coming of the new organization', *Harvard Business Review*, Jan/Feb.

Garratt, B (1990) *Learning to Lead: Developing your Organization and Yourself*, Director Books, New York.

Handy, C (1989) *The Age of Unreason*, Hutchinson.

LGMB (1996) *A Guide to Action Learning for Local Government Managers*, LGMB, London.

Pedler, M (1992) *Action Learning in Practice*, Gower, Aldershot.

Pedler, M, Burgoyne, J and Boydell, J (1991) *The Learning Company. A strategy for sustainable development*, McGraw-Hill, Maidenhead.

Prahalad, C K and Hamel, G (1990) 'The core competence of the corporation', *Harvard Business Review*, May/June.

Senge, P (1990) *The Fifth Discipline*, Century Business, London.

Talbot, C (1997) *Towards a Public Service Excellence Model Discussion Paper.*

9 Individual and team performance

Next generation management will be about results-oriented people and organizations. The organizations will invest appropriately in their employees, recognizing that they are the most flexible and adaptable resource within the authority. Combined with knowledge, an appropriate level of development and training for employees will make a significant contribution to the performance of a Council. Development and training will happen on and off the job and will be identified through systematic processes and pragmatic approaches, ensuring that they are undertaken in the context of service needs and the Council's policy priorities.

Individual and team performance is the sixth arena of the new performance management framework. Individuals alone do not contribute a significant increase in performance. Teams working together with shared values, objectives and common missions, commitment to the service and understanding of their markets is what makes a real difference. Empowered and trusted, equipped and supported by the creation of the right culture, teams will be able to survive a great deal of turbulence.

This chapter will explain how managers in local government are beginning to work in new forms of teams on a cross-service and inter-agency basis across sectors. We will see from these ways of working that people and processes are more important than organization structures. Eventually, structures can and will impede service quality and high performance.

Psychological approaches such as neuro-linguistic programming (NLP) and transactional analysis (TA) are described, along with their potential contribution to creating high performing organizations.

The concepts of fractal and holonic management and virtual teams are discussed. Leading-edge managers will display a high level of energy as they care about what they are doing and believe in their part in it. Leading-edge managers will develop a sensitivity to the language they use to motivate others, and know what triggers high levels of energy in other managers and staff, enabling them to make a greater contribution.

WHAT A HIGH PERFORMANCE WORKPLACE LOOKS LIKE

Roger Woodgate, as a part of his Harkness Fellowship to the USA in 1995, researched elements of high performing organizations among a wide range of American companies. The key features he discovered are:

- small work groups managing the work process;
- flat organization – few management levels; direct access to the leadership team;
- managers facilitating work groups to get the job done, not managing in a traditional way;
- problem solving at the point of delivery;
- shared leadership, not emanating from one person but from many;
- self-managing teams with little direct supervision;
- two-way feedback and communication on progress towards goals between various parts of the business;
- core resource of generalists who are adaptable and who could manage a range of job roles.

HOLONIC TEAMS, FRACTAL ORGANIZATIONS AND VIRTUAL TEAMS

Holonic teams

A number of international organizations and countries are involved in a collaborative research programme to do with intelligent manufacturing systems (IMS). The IMS programme sponsors six projects, including one on holonic manufacturing systems.

Not much of what local government does is concerned with manufacturing. However, much can be learnt from the processes and techniques that are used. After all, quality circles, total quality management, benchmarking and service chain analysis are all techniques that originated in the private sector (particularly manufacturing). Nearly all of the work on holonics has been undertaken in the USA. Arthur Koestler used the term 'holon' in his book *The Ghost in the Machine* (1967) to describe a basic unit of organization in biological and social systems. 'Holos' in Greek is the word for whole and 'on' is a part, such as in 'neutron'. Therefore 'holon' can refer to the interrelationships and connectedness between the parts and the whole.

> The strength of a holonic organization, or holarcy, is that it enables the construction of very complex systems that are efficient in the use of resources, highly resilient to disturbances (both internal and external), and adaptable to changes in the environment in which they exist. The

stability of holons stems from their being self-reliant units, which have a degree of independence and handle circumstances and problems on their particular level of existence without asking higher level holons for assistance. Holons can also receive instruction from and, to a certain extent, be controlled by higher level holons. 'The self-reliant characteristic ensures that holons are stable, able to survive disturbances. The subordination to high level holons ensures the effective operation of the larger whole' (Savage, 1992).

Although research into holonics is in its early stages and concerned with the private sector, I believe that the principles emerging will be transferable to next generation management within local government. The key themes arising from the literature on holonics are to do with autonomy and coordination – key features for teams in next generation management.

Fractal organizations

The Fraunhofer Institute in Germany published *The Fractal Company, A revolution in corporate culture* (Savage, 1992). The concept of fractal enterprises was developed independently, but has a lot of similarities with the idea of holonic management.

A fractal organization is one which has many task-focused teams in knowledge-based networks. Each of the units is unique in character and at the same time understands the overall organization. Each unit is autonomous by way of its organization and its design, but is in line with the organization's mission. These units do not wait to be told what to do: they scan their environments, understand the mission, analyse the situation and communicate with other units, optimizing the operation of their business and their organization as a whole. Every unit is responsible for connecting its own work with the rest of the organization. This snap-shot of thinking on fractal enterprises gives us many clues in terms of the philosophy, management and direction in which networked organizations with empowered staff are moving. Figure 8.5 in the previous chapter could be seen as a good illustration of this type of organization.

Virtual teams

Virtual teams are units of staff who are brought together from across the organization to undertake tasks. Members of the team may well be serving on a range of other teams within the organization. The virtual team would usually have a core member or members of staff who are joined by a wide range of professionals and generalists. The virtual team may be time-limited or indeed a more long term proposition to meet a service need. Virtual teams reflect the characteristics of holonic and fractal management, ie they have a great deal of autonomy and are about coordination of work. Virtual teams must not be mistaken for task groups, which have been established by many local authorities, nor should they be mistaken for matrix management working.

CASE STUDY: THE SCHOOL GOVERNOR DEVELOPMENT UNIT

ESSEX COUNTY COUNCIL

In 1998 Essex CC won a National Top Team Award for their development and piloting of an advance BTEC Certificate in partnership with the Learning from Experience Trust, Essex Training and Enterprise Council and staff from other LEA services.

The judging panel, consisting of nine chief executives and senior directors from the world of local government, gave the award to Essex because it was a virtual team, and as such amongst the most difficult to create and maintain. The special characteristic of this virtual team was that members, organizations and functions within the Council were bonded together as a team by the objectives they agreed to share, rather than the more standard ties of shared organization, culture and location.

This virtual team consisted of:

- core team – full-time team leader;
- part-time external contracted specialist;
- extended team – voluntary (school governors);
- partners (BTEC, Learning from Experience Trust).

In the words of the judges, the team delivered excellent value in key areas of local authority responsibility and service, including:

- better school governors and better school governance;
- more effective partnership between schools, community and local authority;
- directly tested against and responsive to front-line need;
- best practice which can be readily shared within Essex and other local authorities;
- excellent cost/benefits.

The Essex County Council's school governor development team is a good example of a virtual team.

In developing ideas and ways of tackling the best value regime, I have come across a number of local authorities which are creating virtual teams. Many of the virtual team members have specific responsibilities and expertise from the development of performance management systems, market testing, bench-marking, area working and consultation mechanisms. The teams consist of individuals who have been brought together from across the Council and from other agencies with defined values as to how they will work and interrelate their activities and strategies to ensure that a best value culture is created. Some of these teams are time-limited, others are on-going until their job is completed. They are autonomous in that they have to assess their environment, and make decisions on what to do next and how to relate it to the rest of the organization. However, they are also about coordination and networking with other teams to understand what is going on so that work is synchronized across their organizations to achieve best value.

Virtual teams, holonic teams and fractal teams have originated from different parts of the world, but there are some common themes emerging:

- knowledge;
- information;
- the need to assess the environment and make decisions to move forward;
- sharing leadership and responsibility for ways of working for the team and for the organization as a whole;
- being autonomous;
- coordinating and collaborating with others.

These are all elements that also describe next generation management. A comparison of traditional and next generation management teams is shown in Table 9.1.

CASE STUDY: CROSS-FUNCTIONAL TEAM WORKING

LONDON BOROUGH OF HILLINGDON

This case study examines Hillingdon's extensive use of cross-functional teams as a means of resolving corporate problems and as a device for main-taining staff in the early 1990s.

Hillingdon lost around one-third of its total revenue budgets in the early 1990s. This was a profound shock to the system, threatening a collapse in staff morale and trust. The controlling group decided, in light of this, to twin-track the budget cuts with a wider change-management and devolution process, designed to rebuild basic capacities.

One of the main aims of the change-management process was to foster joint problem solving across service delivery units and throughout the decision making hierarchy, through corporate teams. Eight teams were established in the first instance. These teams were intended to be task-oriented: each was set discrete objectives and was to be time-limited. Their performance was judged as enormously productive. New teams were therefore founded, even while some of the original eight were disbanded.

Two distinct approaches to team working have emerged over time: corporate teams, operating to finite objectives and with a finite life-span; and standing groups, with open-ended agendas, often dealing with potentially sensitive issues of representation, communication and consultation. Teams have fostered a great deal of innovation and sharing of good practice at Hillingdon; many of these ideas emanated from third-tier and front-line staff. These contributions have not gone unnoticed or unrewarded, with some individuals enjoying rapid promotion in part due to their team contributions.

Multi-functional local authorities usually over-emphasize the importance of formal organizational structures compared to the more intangible networks and coalitions that tend to matter a great deal more to staff. Hillingdon's approach, combining devolution with corporate team working, has attempted to weave the formal and informal, visible and invisible networks of the authority into a more cohesive whole. The benefits of teams are clear in terms of enhanced innovation and morale-building. Implementing team working has required continuing management commitment and the development of new collaborative skills at all levels.

(Source: LGMB).

THE BELBIN TEAM ROLE TYPES

A collection of individuals makes up a team. In any team, the roles that are adopted and the balance of individuals play an essential part in whether the team is high performing and successful in terms of its task and mission. Belbin (1981) in his book, *Management Teams: Why they succeed or fail*, lists eight role types that team members adopt. They are discussed below to help you analyse your own role and therefore your own contribution, and the role types of others within teams you lead or work in.

The implementer (I)

This is the essential team member because the individual's goals are identical to the team's goals. The I is often the managing director, who performs the task which others do not always want to perform. The I plans systematically and efficiently to transform plans into workable activities.

Table 9.1 *Traditional teams and next generation management (adapted from Woodgate, 1995)*

Element	Traditional Teams	Next Generation Management – Teams
Structure	Hierarchical/controlling	Flat/autonomous
Job design	Narrow, specialists, rigid job boundaries	Whole process, generalists, flexible workers
Management role	Directing, controlling	Coaching, facilitating
Leadership	Top-down	Shared
Adaptability	Trickle down, slow to implement	Interactive, quick dynamic
Information flow	Controlled, limited, one-way	Open, shared, all-directional
Rewards	Individual recognition, seniority	Team recognition, skills-based
Job process	Manager's plans control, approve	Team's plan, control, improve, coordinate, autonomous
Morale	Low, mistruct 'hired hands'	Empowered, trust, 'ownership'

The team-building style of the I is to organize operations. They can lack flexibility and be unresponsive to unproven ideas.

The coordinator (C)

The coordinator organizes team operations and resources for meeting group objectives. The C is clear about the team's strengths and weaknesses and works to maximize each member's potential. The C is good at managing people. The main personality characteristic of the C is strong basic dominance and a commitment to group goals. The C is the calm, unflappable, self-disciplined, encouraging, supportive face of the team leader.

The team-building style of the C is to welcome contributions and evaluate them against team objectives. They are not especially high on intellectual or creative ability.

The shaper (SH)

This is the manipulative, ambitious, entrepreneurial, opportunistic face of team leadership. The SH makes things happen and shapes the team efforts through establishing objectives and priorities. The SH subscribes to the view that winning is the name of the game and, in true Machiavellian style, will resort to illicit or immoral tactics if necessary. Belbin's research found that this is the most preferred team role.

The team-building style of the SH is to challenge, motivate and achieve. They are prone to provocation, irritation and impatience.

The plant (PL)

This is the introverted, intelligent, innovative member. The PL presents new ideas and strategies. The PL is interested in major, wider issues, which may result in a lack of attention to detail.

The team-building style of the PL is to bring innovative ideas to team operations, activities and goals. They are apt to be 'up in the clouds' and inclined to disregard details or protocol.

The resource investigator (RI)

This is the extroverted, resource-gathering face of the plant. The RI explores and reports on ideas, resources and new developments which occur outside the team. The RI is a natural at public relations and creates useful external contacts for the team. The RI usually knows how to match people with common interests, and who can help to solve problems.

The team-building style of the RI is to network and gather useful resources for the team. They may lose interest once the initial fascination has passed.

The monitor-evaluator (ME)

The ME is objective at analysing problems and evaluating ideas. Rarely carried away by enthusiasm, the ME prevents the team from making impulsive, foolhardy decisions.

The team-building style of the ME is to objectively analyse and evaluate team ideas and decisions. They may lack inspiration or the ability to motivate others.

The team worker (TW)

The TW plays a relationship-oriented, supportive role. The TW is a highly popular type and is not uncommon among top managers; this is because the TW is highly sociable with low dominance needs. The TW fosters team spirit, improves interpersonal communications and minimizes interpersonal conflict within the team.

The team-building style of the TW is to support relationships within the team. They can be indecisive at moments of crisis.

The completer-finisher (CF)

The CF is concerned with progress and perseveres with the project when the excitement and enthusiasm of the other members have waned. The CF is a good planner, implementer and achiever of team tasks. The CF is irritated if work falls behind schedule and loses job satisfaction when jobs are not completed.

The team-building style of the CF is to press for progress, meeting deadlines and task completion, and they are reluctant to 'let go'.

Competency profiling

In earlier chapters we have discussed many of the competencies associated with leading-edge managers who will be working in new local government. Competencies are the relevant qualities, skills and abilities that lead to effective performance.

The main benefit of competency profiling is in establishing clear, measurable standards that are used to improve the performance of the organization through:

- recruiting and selecting competent staff;
- appraising and recognizing performance in the job against clear objectives;
- identifying the training and development needs of individuals;
- planning organization development programmes.

The idea of competency has its origins in psychological theory. The modern competence movement originates from the work of David McClelland, founder of the McBer (later Hay McBer) Consultancy in the United States. In 1973 McClelland argued that 'traditional academic examinations did not predict job performance or success in life, and were often biased against minorities, women and other groups'. He argued people should instead be looking for 'competencies' that could predict success and that were less biased. For McClelland a competency is an underlying personal characteristic that causes effective or superior performance in any given situation. These competencies reflect motives, traits, skills, self-image, and bodies of knowledge which people use to operate effectively in performing specified roles. The competencies are recognized and described in terms of what people do or the way they behave. The basic approach developed by Hay McBer has been to identify the way successful or superior performers in particular jobs or roles behave. This analysis produces a template that people can use as a model for recruiting or training and developing people. Every job profile will contain a number of competencies (usually between 12 and 20) each with its own narrative description and set of behavioural indicators.

Close to the Hay McBer approach in the UK has been the Management Charter Initiative (MCI). Along with the notion of occupational standards, the MCI has also developed 'personal effectiveness competencies' which bear a good deal of resemblance to Boyatzis' *The Competent Manager* (1982). The MCI has been adopted by a wide range of organizations in both the private and public sectors as a way of developing and accrediting managerial competencies. While some organizations have found it detailed, thorough and challenging, others have found it too generic, bureaucratic and time-consuming.

At the end of the day next generation management will use a competence framework only if it gives them the information they need in an accessible and relevant format. While there may be competence requirements that are common for all leading-edge managers, the way those competencies are expressed and the standards they describe (whether it is excellence or minimum requirements) will vary considerably between local authorities. This is why many organizations have chosen to produce their own competence frameworks that embody the values, standards and culture they want to develop.

Whichever approach is adopted, the purpose of the competence framework is to describe the competencies that are important to the local authority as a whole and are required to do specific jobs or roles within the organization. The competencies are described in terms of the 'actions' that are essential for the organization and for job holders to be successful. A job description usually describes 'what' a person is expected to do or achieve. A competence profile describes 'how' those duties, responsibilities or outcomes should be achieved. How the actions are worded will depend on what is important, what standards are being aimed for, and how much detail people need for the information to be useful.

Using behavioural statements provides organizations with a powerful common language that can be used to describe roles or jobs and the performance of the people who are doing them. Competencies provide a tool for assessing how organizations, teams and individuals are behaving compared to the behaviour that is desired or required. This comparison can then inform staff development meetings and training programmes, personal development, recruitment, selection and organizational development activities.

Competence frameworks can be developed by following these basic steps:

- establishing or reaffirming the purpose and objectives of your organization;
- determining the key competencies needed within the organization to achieve the objectives;
- identifying the jobs/roles to be performed;
- describing the actions or behaviours people will demonstrate when performing effectively in the role.

Task 9.1

What are the key competencies for leading-edge managers in the new local government context?

TRANSACTIONAL ANALYSIS AND HIGH PERFORMING 'BLAME-FREE' CULTURES

What is transactional analysis (TA)?

TA is a theory of personality and communication that provides methods for personal change and improving communication, and offers powerful tools for organizational analysis. It is based on the work of Eric Berne, author of *The Games People Play*, and best known for its ego-state model of parent–adult–child. This helps explain how people are structured psychologically: how sometimes we behave like a copy of one of our parents (our parent ego state); at other times as a grown-up person (our adult ego state); and sometimes in the way we used to when a child (our child ego state).

One of the philosophical underpinnings of TA is that people are ok. This means that you and I both have worth, value and dignity as people. I accept myself as me and I accept you as you. At times I may not like nor accept what you *do*, but I always accept what you *are*. Your essence as a human being is ok with me, even though your behaviour may not be.

Blame is pervasive in organizations. Indeed even in the absence of anyone blaming us for our mistakes or for less-than-perfect performance, we tend to blame ourselves! The significance of blaming is that there is a cycle which leads to a downward spiral (see Figure 9.1).

Figure 9.1   *The blame cycle (Momentum Consultants, 1998)*

165

The principle that people are ok offers a way out of the blame culture. The work of Franklin Ernst gives next generation managers a way of thinking about organizations, teams and individuals which can enable them to create a culture of empowerment – an important element of high performing organizations.

TA suggests that humans make fundamental decisions about themselves and others in the first few years of life, particularly in relation to whether they think of themselves as ok or not ok, and whether they think of others as ok or not ok. These fundamental decisions become beliefs and determine the individual's behaviour.

If a person fundamentally thinks of themselves as not ok and others as ok, then they will continually discount their own performance and look to others for support and help – they act the 'victim', feel inadequate and have very little self-confidence.

Someone who believes that they are ok and others are not either gets irritated with others and acts the 'persecutor' – criticizing and blaming; or alternatively feels sympathy for others and acts as a 'rescuer' – helping and doing things for them. Both 'persecutor' and 'rescuer' have a very comfortable relationship with 'victims' as they support each other's fundamental views of the world: I'm ok and you're not; I'm not ok and you are. This dynamic is the basis for many relationships, both inside and outside work, which while comfortable are unproductive.

Some people believe that neither they nor others are ok and the situation is hopeless. In an organizational context, this is the type of person who thinks you should keep your head down and wait for early retirement!

Finally, there is the person who believes they are ok and so are other people; that everyone has the potential to perform and develop, and may not yet have had the training to equip them with the skills they need. This is the domain of being straight and direct with people, respectfully being assertive, and having a fundamental belief in others – the place of empowerment.

In practice Ernst said that we all move around these different life positions, although under pressure we tend to revert to the one we feel most comfortable with. The goal is to spend as much of our time as possible in 'I'm ok, you're ok'.

How 'I'm ok, you're ok' can be used to improve individual and team performance

Managing performance using 'I'm ok, you're ok' involves making a distinction between a person's identity, which is of course ok, and their behaviour, which may not be useful. One can then focus on the desired behaviour without blaming or criticizing the person, so as to avoid hooking the person's 'victim'.

The behaviour or action wanted can be talked through objectively, focusing on the relevant facts, the options and the implications of different courses of action. In consequence, the parties avoid feelings associated with being a persecutor, rescuer or victim.

It is important for managers to be aware that there is already some 'I'm ok, you're not' in the system by virtue of the organization's hierarchy. A manager is higher up the hierarchy than members of staff and therefore by implication more ok than them. Chief executives become the most ok person around, which helps explain why so few people challenge them!

This means that managers need to act in a very conscious way to encourage 'I'm ok, you're ok' in their teams and so create a culture of empowerment. Staff will then see themselves as on the same level as managers, just having different roles. They can then be encouraged to come up with their own ideas and approaches, and to apply clear thinking to tasks and problem solving.

Empowerment and a blame-free culture cannot be created over night. Many organizations and managers seem to think that they can just ask employees for their own ideas and they will miraculously become empowered. When they do not immediately spout forth suggestions, this is taken as evidence that empowerment does not work. However, with investment in training and conscious attention to encouraging 'I'm ok, you're ok', a culture of empowerment and continual improvement can be created. This involves training for managers and employees on how they can spend more of their time in 'I'm ok, you're ok', combined with continual encouragement and reinforcement through day-to-day management and staff development. There is then more energy spent on achieving results and solving problems, and lesson blaming, back-covering and game-playing.

NEURO-LINGUISTIC PROGRAMMING (NLP)

What is NLP?

Neuro-linguistic programming is the study of how people excel in any field and how to teach these patterns to other people, so they too can get the same results. This process is called modelling. NLP covers not only modelling but also the models that are created. These patterns, skills and techniques are being used increasingly in management, counselling and education for more effective communication, accelerated learning and personal development. Leading-edge managers need to learn rapidly how to deal with an ever-changing environment. NLP can help them to become more productive.

The title 'neuro-linguistic programming' represents the three areas that NLP has brought together:

● 'neuro' refers to our neurology – our thinking processes;

- 'linguistic' is language – how we use it and how we are influenced by it;
- 'programming' refers to the patterns of our behaviour and the goals we set.

NLP relates our words, thoughts and behaviour to our goals.

Why NLP is relevant to next generation management

Next generation management is about excelling in all fields of management to achieve high performance. NLP offers a way of replicating excellence, of taking the most effective approaches to communicating, developing and bringing about change, and making these available to managers.

A selection of NLP approaches that next generation management will want available include:

- how to align an organization's vision and mission with its culture, its people's capabilities and what people do in order to harness the full potential of its workforce;
- how to set goals that are far more likely to be achieved ('well formed outcomes');
- how to communicate goals in such a way that presupposes success and hence increases success (the use of presuppositions);
- how to communicate effectively to match the different ways people think (images, sounds, words and feelings);
- how to build rapport with even the most difficult people;
- how to take different perspectives to improve communication and analysis by gathering different sources of information (first perspective as your own reality, second perspective as another's reality and third perspective as the systemic overview of both);
- how to gather information through precise questions about what underpins a person's words;
- how to stay resourceful whatever the challenge facing you.

Many managers will be familiar with the SMART approach to goal setting (Specific, Measurable, Achievable, Relevant and Time-targeted). NLP provides a way of making objectives measurable, even when dealing with qualitative performance such as someone's behaviour.

Reality for humans is comprised of three sets of data: visual, auditory (sounds and words) and feelings (both internal and external sensations). Describing what you will see, hear and feel when you've reached your goal provides a way of making the goal clearer and of knowing when the goal is achieved. It can also be used to clarify the behaviour wanted from a member of staff.

Focusing on the positive

So often employees are told what not to do rather than what is wanted in the future. Managers find it easier to describe the see, hear, feel data in front of them ('Don't be late!') rather than what they want to be different ('Arrive on time!').

NLP places emphasis on using language that focuses on what is wanted, rather than what is not, because the mind creates pictures and sounds as a result of the language it hears. For example 'Don't think about a blue kangaroo' can only be made sense of by first thinking about a blue kangaroo which we then metaphorically draw a line through. Research has found that most slipping accidents happen under signs instructing people 'Don't slip'. Seeing that, what is the picture you have in your mind? Don't slip, don't slip, don't ... oops!

Negative language (don'ts) also has an effect on our emotional state. Hearing a series of don'ts tends to make us depressed. Not only does this sort of language encourage people to focus on exactly what is not wanted, it also makes them miserable! Hence next generation managers will be very careful in the language they use – an NLP saying is 'You get what you focus on, so focus on want you want'.

TEAM APPRAISAL AND DEVELOPMENT

Changes in organization culture and structures, flattened hierarchies and greater emphasis on team working, cross-service and inter-agency working, and managers with a greater span of control have all led to the emergence of team appraisal or 360 degree feedback systems. These are most often used as one of several tools in the process of identifying development needs to bridge performance gaps. They are rarely tied to decisions on pay.

Team appraisal can ensure collective effort rather than a focus on individual performance. This can also bring benefits in groups where individuals generally have their own tasks and the collaboration needed is minimal (in what some people distinguish as work groups as opposed to work teams) – it ensures a focus on team effort.

One approach is to assign a lead person responsible for each goal/task, who leads the review at team meetings (typically quarterly reviews). The team leader's role becomes one of ensuring sufficient resources are available for the task and agreeing priorities as necessary.

Probably the most effective way of using competencies within team appraisals is to use them in addition to establishing progress towards goals, targets and standards. The person then self-reviews against the competence description (profile) with feedback from the manager and others in the team.

If the competence description/profile is used in isolation, there is a risk that you will focus on activities rather than results.

Synchrony, designed by Development Dimensions International (DDI), uses a comprehensive three-step process. These steps involve collecting data on the individuals and groups, interpreting reports, then supporting individual and group development plans. Applying a multiple rate format, synchrony gathers information from the person being assessed and the individual's peers, subordinates and boss. State-of-the-art software analyses the data and produces a range of easy-to-interpret profiles that describe the strengths and development needs of individuals and groups in relation to the requirements of the job, and allows for targeting of priority programmes or interventions. The multi-rate format improves the objectivity of the evaluations and provides comparisons between the self-assessment and assessment by others.

In 1998 The Industrial Society launched its Liberating Leadership Profile. It allows management teams at all levels to benchmark themselves against a 38-point profile. The most important element is the upward feedback reports. The profile exercise is totally confidential and each manager/group leader profiled receives feedback on the 38 points. Many of these are likely to be straightforward to address. Group profiles of management teams reveal patterns for the team as a whole and indicate where the organization's own procedures and practices fall short, allowing dialogue on how best to improve leadership within the team and overall organizational performance. The profiling exercise provides a benchmark and enables decisions to be made about training and development needs. The Liberating Leadership Profile is an excellent aid to improving individual and team performance. Dr Warren Bennis, international leadership guru, says 'the measures The Industrial Society has developed for profiling and measuring leaders and leadership are the best I have seen anywhere'.

The benefits of team appraisal and development for the organization are:

- identifying the strengths of individuals or groups which might be under-utilized;
- providing data for succession-planning discussions;
- ascertaining the particular development needs of disadvantaged groups within the organization;
- matching individual's skills to those of a group, for example to form a clearer foundation for effective team development.

SUMMARY

In this chapter we have considered how culture and the shape of our organizations can facilitate the emergence of new types of teams, contributing to higher levels of performance. This chapter emphasizes the need for next generation management to consider new ways of organizing work teams to meet the needs of citizens, learning from others. Leading-edge managers in charge of work teams consisting of members from different services and sectors will need to understand the dynamics of teams and the contribution of individuals, and utilize leading-edge thinking such as neuro-linguistic programming to help them seek higher levels of performance. New cultures and shapes of organizations will require new ways of identifying performance gaps and measuring achievement.

In Chapter 10 we consider the relationships between quality and performance, and make the links with best value and the new performance management framework. The contribution of quality standards inspection and control mechanisms to a Council's overall performance is also examined.

REFERENCES

Belbin, R M (1981) *Management Teams: Why they succeed or fail*, Butterworth-Heinemann, Oxford.

Boyatzis, R E (1982) *The Competent Manager: A Model for Effective Performance*, Wiley, Chichester.

McClelland (1973) Testing for competence rather that intelligence, *American Psychological Journal*, **28**.

Momentum Consultants (1998) *The Blame Cycle*, training material, Momentum Consultants, York.

Savage, C (1992) *Fifth Generation Management: Co-creating through virtual enterprises, dynamic teaming and knowledge networking*, Butterworth and Hienmann, London.

Woodgate, R (1995) *The High Performance Organization. What does it look like and how do you make it happen?*, Harkness Fellowship Report, London.

10 Quality and the new performance management framework

The purpose of this chapter is to make the links between quality and performance, focusing on quality standards and operational frameworks as outlined in the last quadrant of the new performance management framework in Chapter 3. We will consider what is meant by quality, its relationship to best value, and the different approaches to quality. At the end of the chapter we will review the key issues leading-edge managers need to address in high performing, modern local authorities.

For new local government many of the issues concerned with quality management over the last two decades have merged into aspects of the best value regime in one way or another. Perhaps one of the significant changes is the language used.

The concept of quality has been around for many decades in both the public and private sectors. The most famous names associated with quality are Demming, Duran, Crosby and Ishikawa. Peters and Waterman, authors of *In Search of Excellence* (1992) identified quality as a key to organizational survival in an environment of increasing competition, rising consumer expectations, diminishing resources and rapid economic, social and political change. This scenario fits the challenges that new local government faces in the new millennium.

New local government is about achieving best value for citizens who are also consumers; it must therefore be about quality. In Chapter 5 we discussed best value as a way of working that involves customers as our citizens in identifying their needs, hopes and expectations, and in judging how well we have performed in meeting their needs.

Leading-edge managers must understand what quality is and its contribution to providing best value for new local government. In Chapter 3, in the overall performance management framework, we outlined the importance of quality to that framework. Over the last two decades local authorities have witnessed many quality initiatives come and go – and even reappear – but very few, if any, survive in their original form. It is therefore essential that

172

next generation management does not focus on quality management as an isolated subject matter, but rather as a set of tools and techniques and as a part of performance management.

WHAT IS QUALITY?

For many years now, quality within the local government environment has been compared with private sector organizations. As local government increasingly moves into an inter-agency approach and mixed economy of service provision, comparison has been less problematic. More specifically, approaches such as the Business Excellence Model (Chapter 7) facilitate the comparison of performance of different aspects of services across any sector and with any business.

While the experiences of the private sector provide important lessons for new local government, there are many challenges in applying a purely private sector approach:

● It concentrates upon a relationship with individuals as consumers alone. This should not be applied to local authority services as it neglects the relationship with citizens as members of a community to whom local authorities have a collective responsibility and accountability.
● It does not recognize the statutory restraints under which local authorities have to operate, which can limit choices and restrict the delivery of quality services.
● It concentrates upon the users of services, perhaps to the detriment of non-users who may be seeking a totally different type and/or level of service. Access to services is a major issue for local government, particularly for those who have been socially excluded.

The LGMB, in its publication, *Quality: A councillors guide* (1992) provides the following definition of quality: 'Providing services that match the policy commitments of the authority and meet the needs of the service user and community economically, effectively, efficiently and equitably'.

Quality does not necessarily imply increasing levels of service – it means making sure that whatever is provided is done so in the best possible way. The pursuit of quality can focus on future development and can be about:

● improved services;
● gaining a better knowledge of people's needs and experiences of services;
● making sure that policies are actually being implemented;
● finding better ways of delivering services;
● involving service users;

- knowing how successful the authority is in meeting its objectives;
- gaining a competitive edge in trading services.

The development of a quality approach in local government has been about the continual improvement of services. So what is the difference between approaches to quality in local government over the previous two decades and best value now?

Forms of quality

To answer this question I will need to refer back to the description of the new performance management framework in Chapter 3. Here we see that the traditional tools and techniques associated with quality management are contained in only one quadrant of the framework: the one concerning 'operational control'. On the other hand, the principles and facts associated with best value can be seen in all four quadrants of the framework. From this we see that best value is a much more holistic approach to achieving quality in the new local government context.

There are three forms which an approach to quality can take:

1. *Quality control.* Monitoring services to ensure that agreed standards are being met, for example by reviewing performance against targets, or through direct inspection as in schools or Social Services residential establishments.
2. *Quality assurance.* Developing management systems that ensure good quality services are delivered. Quality assurance includes the attempt to get services right first time and avoid mistakes. It will involve considering issues such as the design of services, the processes of service delivery and the way in which faults and mistakes are dealt with. Such an approach will include quality control measures.
3. *Total quality management (TQM).* Creating a commitment to continual service improvement within the authority. TQM involves an attempt to change the culture and strategy of the organization to emphasize everyone's contribution to effective performance, and will include both quality control and quality assurance approaches.

There are three elements to my definition of quality:

- Does the product or service conform to specification?
- Is it fit for its purpose? (Does it do what it's supposed to do?)
- Does it meet the agreed requirements of the service user?

Other contemporary definitions of quality include delighting the customer; satisfying the customer; zero defects and right first time.

Quality and the new performance management framework

The new performance management framework is not definitive or static. It is a map that local government managers can use to diagnose where they are currently focusing their energies, resources, systems and processes to achieve high performance. It is also a framework for mapping out a journey to achieve high performance and modernization for local government. It can be used to diagnose where there are performance gaps and as a tool for envisioning ways of improving performance. Quality management, the associated tools, techniques and operational frameworks, make a contribution to a coherent and holistic approach to improving performance.

In the 1980s the whole emphasis on achieving higher quality services for customers was based on using quality assurance, quality control and TQM approaches. However, if next generation managers focus exclusively or too strongly on these ways of working, less attention will be paid to other aspects of the best value and modernization agenda, in particular citizen participation. Achieving high performance and becoming a modern local authority will require local authorities to focus their attention on all four quadrants of the new performance management framework:

- civic leadership and democracy – citizens and performance; political management;
- strategic planning – performance; information and measuring performance;
- results-oriented people – organizational performance; individual and team performance;
- operational control – quality standards; operational frameworks.

THE TOOLS AND TECHNIQUES ASSOCIATED WITH QUALITY

There many tools and techniques described in a plethora of quality management literature. In many local authorities such a wide range of tools and techniques are used that rarely is learning captured and little time is spent on analysing the best methods for specific environments. A key benefit of focusing on a smaller number of techniques for improving performance is being able to develop standards for the methods used, ensuring consistency of application. This will help everyone to understand the way in which improvement teams at all levels can tackle and report back on their tasks. The toolbox of techniques ranges from basic analytical and problem solving methods to more complex approaches such as value chain analysis (Porter, 1985) and the balanced score card method (Kaplan and Norton, 1996). Although this chapter does not cover these approaches in any depth, they are outlined below.

Statistical process control (SPC)

Although this may sound incredibly complex, SPC problem solving for quality improvement requires the use of some very straightforward tools and techniques that most people will be familiar with. Some of them are described below.

Pareto analysis

The 80/20 rule under which data is collected and sorted to identify the most frequent causes of a problem. Remedial action is then focused on the more significant.

Flowcharts

These present a picture of the key elements in a process. By comparing what happens with what *should* happen, sources of difficulty can be uncovered.

Control charts

The collection of objective evidence of areas, processes and outputs that are not meeting customer requirements and the action that needs to be taken. This is frequently best carried out in collaboration with customer/suppliers.

Cause and effect analysis

This is often used in support of brainstorming sessions and is a concise way of setting out the causes of a problem by linking them in diagrammatic form. The diagram is usually compiled by one person writing up the ideas of others in a group session. When well prepared it looks like a fish bowl – the name often used for the diagram.

Scatter diagrams

These are used to investigate and illustrate the correlation between two factors.

Value chain analysis

The concept of the value chain was introduced by Porter (1985) in his book on competitive advantage. The value chain is a way of looking at a firm's activities to enable it to identify sources of competitive advantage.

In their report, *Made to Measure – Evaluation in practice in local government*, Sanderson *et al* (1998) put forward a simplified service value chain; this is shown in Figure 10.1. They indicate that performance can be analysed in terms of different elements of the value chain. The notion of a value chain can be applied by thinking of the authority's delivery of a service as a process of producing value for customers and citizens. The process can be disaggregated into a chain of elements whose value can be defined and measured – this can provide a comprehensive framework for the evaluation of services.

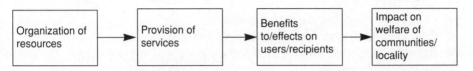

Figure 10.1 *A simplified service value chain*

The balanced score card

Kaplan and Norton, in their book *Translating Strategy into Action – A balanced score card* (1996), describe how the balanced score card method can guide the current performance of an organization and target future performance. They show how to use measures in four categories – financial performance; customer knowledge; internal business processes; and learning and growth – to align individual, organizational and cross-departmental initiatives and to identify entirely new processes for meeting customer and shareholder objectives. The balanced score card approach emerged from a multi-company study on 'measuring performance in the organization of the future'.

A driver of this study was the fact that performance measure approaches within the private sector were relying too heavily on financial accounting measures. Primarily a tool designed *by* the private sector *for* the private sector, the balanced score card approach provides a framework to translate a strategy into operational terms, focusing on a much wider range of financial and non-financial performance measures.

Applying quality tools and techniques

Here are the key stages in a quality improvement programme (the major components are also shown in Figure 10.2):

- define the problem;
- gather data and chart the problem;
- identify solutions;
- short term fix;
- take short term action to remedy the effects while you get on and examine the cause of the problem;
- examine the cause;

- use a flowchart to map out key elements in a process;
- construct a cause-and-effect diagram;
- analyse the data using a Pareto diagram to focus attention on major causes;
- brainstorm suggestions for corrective action; select the best one. Benchmarking can add a useful external stimulus;
- implementation;
- ensure adequate resources are available;
- train everyone, gain their commitment and involve them;
- document and communicate progress;
- monitor and review;
- chart progress;
- evaluate effectiveness;
- feedback lessons;
- move on to the next problem.

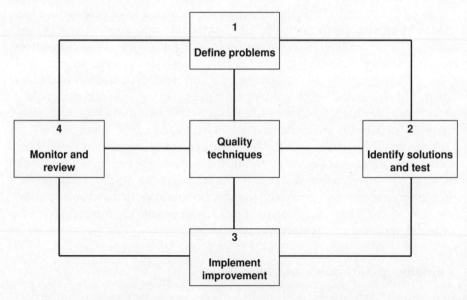

Figure 10.2 *Applying the tools and techniques of quality management*

OPERATIONAL FRAMEWORKS

The eighth and final arena of the new performance management framework concerns operational frameworks such as internal and external audit, zero-based budgeting, statutory inspections undertaken by OFSTED and the Social Services Inspectorate, and competitive tendering. All local authorities will need to implement a wide range of approaches to ensure effective operational control as part and parcel of their holistic approach to performance management. The framework is the 'balanced score card' for next generation management.

Internal and external audit

As a part of the best value regime, the internal and external audit functions of local authorities will become increasingly important. The challenge for new local government is to ensure that internal and external audit procedures are designed in such a way as not to add further layers of bureaucracy that could impede the development of an authority's approach to continuous improvement.

External audit is an independent appraisal function. This independence has its advantages. The external auditor can view the local authority from a more detached stance and, with a wider remit covering other organizations, comparisons and the percolation of ideas between organizations are possible. However, there is the disadvantage of divorcing the auditor from the internal system of communication and information. Internal auditors will be primarily responsible to management within the local authority, while the external auditor is a product of statue.

Internal audit is an integral part of the financial structure of the local authority. Over the years the precise role of internal audit has changed. Today it is about more than just the prevention and detection of errors and fraud (although these are important): auditors operate in a fast changing, complex environment with a heavy emphasis on reviewing systems of internal control. There are some notable examples of local authorities that have divested their internal audit functions and suffered the consequences!

Zero-based budgeting (ZBB)

ZBB is a cost/benefit approach whereby it is assumed that the cost allowance for an item is zero, and will remain so until the manager responsible justifies the existence of the cost item and the benefits the expenditure brings.

This particular approach is very conducive to the principles of best value where resources expended to make or deliver services need to be challenged and compared, and performance consulted upon and considered against the competition. It brings about a questioning attitude, whereby each cost item has to be justified in terms of how it helps to meet service objectives and how it benefits the authority as a whole. This is a more imaginative and forward-looking approach than incremental budgeting based on historical reasoning.

It is recognized that the principle of ZBB is sound; however, its application in a particular organization may well prove to be difficult if it is applied to *all* budgets. It is considered to be time-consuming and could lead to considerable friction between budget holders. As with other forms of budgeting there are many subjective elements in ZBB and it is susceptible to political pressures. Colleagues working within the financial services sector of local government believe that it should be used selectively in overhead and policy budgets, on a rotational basis. In this way, periodically selected budgets would be subjected to a rigorous scrutiny based on sound principles. The performance management framework for best value illustrated in Figure 5.1 clearly indicates that the rigorous approach associated with ZBB will be a key feature for all service areas under the best value regime.

Statutory inspection procedures

Over recent years local government has been subjected to an ever-increasing range of statutory inspection procedures. OFSTED in education and Social Services Inspectorate/Audit Commission joint reviews of social services are two key examples. There is no question that the government's approach to improving performance within local government and its agenda for revitalizing local government have brought with them both a prescriptive top-down and a flexible bottom-up approach.

Although few schools would wholeheartedly welcome a full OFSTED inspection, regular, external scrutiny within an agreed framework can be used by a school to support, stimulate and guide its own programme of development. It can, for example:

● act as an additional impetus for managing change;
● provide an external check on progress;
● provide an 'audit' of the current position in the school;
● provide feedback, in depth, across a very broad range of school activities;
● confirm, or suggest a revision of, the school's agenda for further development.

The challenge for local government is to synchronize as best as possible local and national time-scales for scrutiny of services and align the tools and techniques used, ensuring energy is not wasted in the journey to becoming a high performing, modern local authority.

CASE STUDY: A COHERENT APPROACH TO PERFORMANCE
NORTH TYNESIDE METROPOLITAN COUNCIL

North Tyneside Council recognized that there was a need to improve their internal performance management processes by widening the scope for members to be involved in questions of the performance of the organization. In 1995 work began on looking at the overall development of the organization, facilitated by the Local Government Centre at Warwick Business School. An additional priority was identified: to establish a coherent corporate policy planning process. The aim was to bring together into a unified

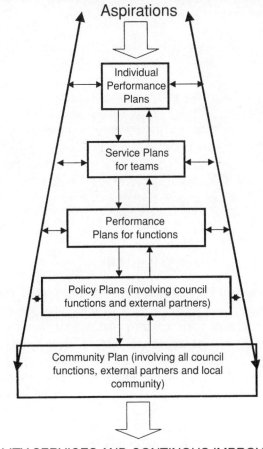

Aspirations

Individual Performance Plans

Service Plans for teams

Performance Plans for functions

Policy Plans (involving council functions and external partners)

Community Plan (involving all council functions, external partners and local community)

QUALITY SERVICES AND CONTINOUS IMPROVEMENT

Figure 10.3   *Quality services and continuous improvement (North Tyneside)*

process the key strategic aims set by members – policy development, service planning, target setting and monitoring. Although initially progress was slow, it has been more rapid since 1997. Figure 10.3 illustrates North Tyneside's approach to achieving quality and continuous improvement through their medium term planning cycle.

Performance management is achieved within this model at several levels:

● Through internal validation – this involves staff development processes created through achieving the Investors in People award, and 360 degree appraisal with the top three layers of the organization, with members taking an active role in the process.
● Through corporate validation – operated through the executive directorate and the scrutiny group of members.
● Through external validation – all services are externally validated through consultative processes as part of the Council's approach to best value.

A scrutiny group of members with political balance has been established as part of new performance management arrangements. It has been important to support the scrutiny role of elected members, through an enhanced team of staff in member's services, greater use of IT, extensive induction training, and regular surveys of member's views and their training and development needs. Community consultation and involvement is underpinned with the continuing development of the representative role of individual members of the Council as a whole.

SUMMARY

This chapter has not taken you through the detailed tools and techniques of quality management; rather it has tried to undertake the complex task of reflecting the interrelationships between quality, best value and an authority's overall approach to performance management. The tools and techniques associated with quality management are still important methods for leading-edge managers. However, they need to be complemented with a range of community participation techniques such as citizens juries and area working (see Chapter 5).

CONCLUSION

Performance management in new local government is no longer an easy and simple task. To achieve the status of a high performing, modern local authority, leading-edge managers need:

- to understand the context of new local government;
- the competencies required to work on a cross-service and inter-agency basis;
- to understand the link between strategy and operations;
- to invest in training and development for themselves and the people working for them;
- strong values of social justice and service quality;
- to be both generalists and specialists;
- to work as leaders and as subordinates in work teams as the situation requires.

As Skipper (1997) indicates, there are four conditions for achieving a comprehensive approach to performance in local authority services:

1. We must know what users expect from our services and to what extent our current provision can meet these expectations.
2. We must have clear standards and targets to measure performance.
3. We must ensure a responsive resource base for the delivery of services to these expectations and to these standards.
4. We must build quality assurance into the service delivery process.

The journey to becoming a high performing local authority will take time. However, it does not require definitive detailed plans: it is an organic process that begins when the first person recognizes that things need to change.

A final thought courtesy of Xerox (1996):

When 99.9% is NOT Good Enough

- One hour of unsafe drinking water each month
- Two unsafe landings per day at O'Hare Airport
- 16,000 pieces of US mail lost every hour
- 20,000 incorrect prescriptions each year
- 500 incorrect surgical operations each week
- 50 newborn babies dropped at birth every day
- 22,000 cheques deducted from the wrong bank account each year

(USA data)

REFERENCES

Kaplan, R S and Norton, D P (1996) *Translating Strategy into Action A balanced score card*, HBS Press, Boston.
LGMB (1992) *Quality: A councillors guide*, LGMB, London.

Peters, T J and Waterman, R H (1992) *In Search of Excellence. Lessons from America's Best Run Companies*, Harper & Row, London.

Porter, M (1985) *Competitive Advantage: Creating and sustaining superior performance*, Free Press, New York.

Sanderson, I, Bovaird, T, Davis, P, Martin, S and Foreman, A (1998) *Made to Measure. Evaluation in practice in local government*, LGMB, London.

Skipper, T (1997) *Quality Counts*, Newsletter of Coventry City Council, June.

Xerox Corp. (1996) *Xerox Quality Training Manual*, Xerox, Uxbridge.

Further reading

Armstrong, M (1994) *Reward Management*, Kogan Page, London.

Best, D P (1996) *The Fourth Resource: Information and its Management*, ASLIB/Gower, Aldershot.

Butterly, R, Hurford, C and Simpson, R K (1993) *Audit in the Public Sector*, ICSA Publishing, London.

Carter, N, Kline, R and Day, P (1992) *How Organisations Measure Success – the use of performance indicators in government*, Routledge, London.

Cook, J A and Saniforth, J (1997) *The Learning Organisation in the Public Services*, Gower, Aldershot.

Edwards, M R and Ewen, A (1996) *360° Feedback: the Powerful New Model for Employee Assessment and Performance Improvement*, Amacom, New York.

Fisher, J G (1996) *How to Improve Performance through Benchmarking*, Kogan Page, London.

Goold, M and Quinn, J (1990) *Strategic Control Milestones for Long Term Performance*, Ashridge Hutchinson, London.

Lipnack, J and Stamps, J (1997) *Virtual Teams. Reaching across space, time and organisations with technology*, Wiley, Chichester.

Morgan, G (1986) *Images of Organisation*, Sage, London.

Neale, F (1991) *The Handbook of Performance Management, Institute of Personnel Management*, IPM, London.

Smith, C and DVaz, G (1996) *Upward and 360° Appraisal*, Institute of Management Foundation, London.

Stewart, J (1995) *Local Government Today*. An observers view, LGMB, London.

Stewart, J (1995) *Understanding the Management of Local Government*, Longman/Local Government Training Board, Harlow.

Walters, M (1995) (reprinted 1997) *The Performance Management Handbook*, Institute of Personnel and Development, London.

Young, K (1997) *Portrait of Change*, LGMB, London.

Index

PM stands for performance management and BC for Borough Council. Most of the entries for specific locations of Councils are under 'case study'. Against page numbers, t *means table and* f *means figure.*

Visit Kogan Page on-line

Comprehensive information on
Kogan Page titles

Features include

- complete catalogue listings,
  including book reviews and
  descriptions

- special monthly promotions

- information on NEW titles and
  BESTSELLING titles

- a secure shopping basket facility
  for on-line ordering

PLUS everything you need to know
about KOGAN PAGE

http://www.kogan-page.co.uk